IMPOSSIBLE TRUTHS

ERICH VON DÄNIKEN
IMPOSSIBLE TRUTHS

WATKINS

Sharing Wisdom Since
1893

IMPOSSIBLE TRUTHS
Erich von Däniken

First published in 2018 by Watkins

This edition published in the UK and USA in 2021 by
Watkins, an imprint of Watkins Media Limited
Unit 11, Shepperton House, 83–93 Shepperton Road
London N1 3DF

enquiries@watkinspublishing.com

PUBLISHER: Etan Ilfeld
TRANSLATOR: Adam Gordon
EDITOR: Judy Barratt
HEAD OF DESIGN: Glen Wilkins
DESIGNER: Luise Roberts
PRODUCTION: Uzma Taj

A CIP record for this book is available from the British Library

ISBN: 978-1-78678-543-5 (Paperback)
ISBN: 978-1-78678-114-7 (eBook)

10 9 8 7 6 5 4 3 2 1

Typeset in News Gothic BT
Colour reproduction by XY Digital
Printed in Turkey

Notes:
Abbreviations used throughout this book:
CE Common Era (the equivalent of AD)
BCE Before the Common Era (the equivalent of BC)

www.watkinspublishing.com

Contents

A LETTER TO MY READERS

My book *Chariots of the Gods?* [102] came out in 1968, some 50 years ago now. It was then that I shook for the first time the edifice of history, archaeology and religion that has been built up over the millennia. Why, I asked, do the artwork and sacred texts of ancient cultures all over the globe appear to depict flying craft and astronauts? How could the medieval Piri Reis map show Earth as our planet is seen from space? What of the prehistoric artefacts that include electrical batteries and cut-crystal lenses that today could only be manufactured by complex electro-chemical processes? What of the cave drawings that replicate with astonishing precision the exact position of the constellations as they were 10,000 years ago? All the evidence pointed in one direction: visitors from other parts of the universe must have brought their technological expertise to Earth in the remote past. *The Stones of Kiribati* [100] followed in 1981, with *The Gods and their Grand Design* appearing a year later [101]. Even the comparatively more recent title *Arrival of the Gods* [49], in which I wrote in detail about "the world's greatest picture book" in the Nazca Desert of Peru, is already 20 years old.

My books sold all around the world, but now there's a new generation of readers who don't know about my theories on the inexplicable stone workings at Sacsayhuamán, above the city of Cuzco in Peru, or about Buritaca 200, the mysterious jungle settlement in the Sierra Nevada of Colombia that I was the first to write about. Every day people say to me: "Buritaca? What's that?" "Sacsayhuamán? Never heard of it." "Nazca? Isn't that the UFO place in Mexico?"

I tell myself that it is as it is, and I can't expect other people to share my interests or want to engage with the same riddles from the past that fascinate me! And yet ...

I am convinced that people will be just as intrigued as I am in these mysteries if the proof is put before them. All a researcher can do to engage a new generation is to present the evidence once more and add to it where possible. So, what has happened in the decades since my books were first published? How has the picture changed? Have we solved the riddles or have we found new evidence that can take us toward a solution?

The truth is that we still haven't solved the riddles. We know today as little as we did 100 years ago about the Tello Obelisk and the Raimondi Stele, both found in the ruins of Chavín de Huántar in Peru. Since I wrote my last books, the jungle city of Buritaca 200 in Colombia has opened up to tourism. And through the research undertaken there, we now know the creation stories of the indigenous Kogi peoples, whose ancestors built the city. We have learned of the four priest–gods who came from the far reaches of the cosmos, and who wore masks when they descended to Earth. As with so many other indigenous traditions, the faces of the gods of the Kogi had to be protected from this planet's atmosphere.

But what of Nazca? Haven't we heard every possible theory on that subject by now? In this book I very briefly outline my ideas about Nazca, for the benefit of readers who haven't seen my previous books. Then I let the 38 pictures of Nazca do the rest of the talking for me. Most of these images have never been published before; all of them will take your breath away. It is incredible how much there is to marvel at in the Peruvian desert. And, as I shall explain, nothing at all in these images fits in with the scientific explanations we already have.

Much less well known than Nazca's images are the gigantic earth drawings that exist by the Aral Sea (between Uzbekistan and Kazakhstan), and in Jordan, Saudi Arabia, Chile and Mexico. It would be a mistake to think that Nazca is unique – that would be to miss the most exciting part of the story. In fact, Nazca is worldwide, as are the ancient descriptions of flying machines found in so many traditions. The earth drawings that can be seen all over the globe are connected – and what connects them is dynamite!

Have you read anything about the meaning of the Tunjo Stones in Colombia? About rocks in Saudi Arabia that have been turned to glass? About a petrified forest in Patagonia, where the logs seem to have been sawn through? There's nothing surprising about sawn logs, until you realize that the sawing must have occurred millennia ago, at a time when neither saws nor human beings as we know them now existed. Did you know that every culture of ancient times can be shown to lie on a 40,000km (24,000-mile) band running around the world? Did you know that Nazca is exactly as far from Giza in Egypt as Giza is from Teotihuacán in Mexico? Or that the distance from Angkor Wat in Cambodia to Nazca is the same as the distance from Mohenjo-Daro in Pakistan to Easter Island in the South Pacific? There is much to think about here!

The world of the distant past is amazing. Studying the archaeological evidence changes our perceptions, raises new questions and throws into doubt the natural course of evolution.

Of course evolution exists – but that's not all there is.

I invite you now to open your mind and immerse yourself in a world of impossible truths!

Yours,
Erich von Däniken

CHAPTER ONE:

From Peru to Jerusalem

On 18 April 1980, I visited the archaeological site at Chavín de Huántar in Peru with three companions. Months before, I had read something in a magazine about this place, a mysterious temple of an unknown culture. I studied a map and worked out that Chavín de Huántar was somewhere high up in the Andes.

That April, I rented a car and at the crack of dawn drove out of Lima on the Panamericana del Norte in the direction of Trujillo, the third most populous city in Peru. In the small town of Pativilca, I turned right toward the mountains. The ascent out of the rusty brown canyon begins in a series of tight serpentine bends and makes a seemingly endless climb to a height of 2,600m (8,500ft) and the last gas station at Cajacay. The road takes you a further 80km (50 miles) to the village of Catac, from where the road becomes a steep, dirt track that leads up to the icy mountain lake of Quericocha. Then, at an altitude of 4,510m (14,800ft), you enter the tunnel of the Kahuish Pass. I say "tunnel", but this is no slick alpine thoroughfare as you would get in Europe. Some 500m (1,650ft) long, the Kahuish Pass is roughly hewn from the mountain rock and full of deep potholes, with glacier water edging its way, half-frozen,

Figure 1: The principal structure at Chavín de Huántar, Peru.

down the passage walls. Once through the tunnel, there's a steep descent into the Mosna Valley. The dirt road winds its way downward, one curve curling into another, like an endless snake. You learn to avert your eyes, because a deadly chasm threatens over the edge of the road. At the tiny village of Machac (at 3,180m/10,400ft) you finally reach the valley floor. The ruins of the village complex of Chavín de Huántar lie neglected by the side of the road.

Figure 3: Granite blocks in the Chavín de Huántar complex.

Figure 2: Chavín de Huántar in the Mosna Valley.

This site really does deserve to be called "mysterious", because no one knows who built it, or has managed to decipher the curious representations on its stelae and walls. In an attempt to classify, archaeologists speak nebulously of a "Chavín Culture", whatever that's supposed to mean. All the ruins together form a surface area of about 13 hectares (32 acres) and most of the site stands upon an artificial stone platform. The principal structure is 73m long and 70m wide (240 by 230ft) and constructed out of granite blocks – the blocks at the bottom are the best preserved **(Figures 1–3)** – resting on well-cut flagstones on a levelled surface. It is obvious that there must have been, at some point in the deep past, a group of masterful engineers at work here.

Figure 4: The main gate at Chavín de Huántar.

The main gate **(Figure 4)** of the complex aligns with the east. Two columns, surmounted by a 9m (30ft) monolith, mark the entrance. As it happens I've never clarified to my own satisfaction what this "main gate" was really supposed to be. Today, several monoliths and a heap of rubble lie behind it, apparently washed up there during flooding. Lying on a deeper level than the overall complex is the Sunken Square **(Figure 5)**. From here, four sets of steps lead out in precisely the four cardinal directions. So where are the secrets that make this site so mysterious?

A network of corridors and smaller spaces exist beneath the main building. This network seems to have functioned as a drainage system to disperse the periodic flooding of two streams. In the southeast flows the small Mosna, and in the northwest the Huacheqsa stream. The latter originates in a high mountain lake, and, when the ice melts, its banks break like bursting dams. Since the time that the area fell into disuse, Chavín de Huántar has been afflicted by

Figure 5: The Sunken Square with sets of steps leading out to the cardinal directions.

several outbreaks of flooding. In 1919 the Peruvian archaeologist Julio C. Tello (1880–1947) carried out extensive excavations. When he returned to the site in 1934, a flood had "destroyed a part of the main wing" [1]. Tello wrote that one third of the complex, which he had seen still intact in 1919, had now been swept away. Many underground corridors and canals had been washed out.

Figures 6–10: Tunnel access points at Chavín de Huántar.

I have crawled along some of these corridors myself. If they don't finish up at a dead end, you eventually re-emerge into daylight in a different part of the site. Sometimes I slid out through circular shaft entrances and via rectangular slits in the tunnel **(Figures 6–10)**.

Figures 11–14: Tunnels at Chavín de Huántar.

The corridor ceilings are formed of monoliths, just like those in the Great Pyramid of Giza in Egypt, and the walls are made up of monolithic blocks **(Figures 11–14)**.

It's in these blocks that we encounter the riddles of Chavín de Huántar. The irregular stone walls were originally covered with carved panels, several of which were still lying on the ground when I visited in April 1980 **(Figure 15)**. Others, washed away by the floods, were deposited outside the temple. But what do they depict?

Figure 15: Carved stone panels detached from tunnel walls.

Figure 16 makes no sense at all. In Figures 17 and 18, the tusk-like teeth of these difficult-to-define beings look identical. Figure 19 reveals a figure holding a rounded object in its fist; and Figure 20, according to expert opinion, is supposed to depict a jaguar. That's

Figure 16: A carved stone panel at Chavín de Huántar.

Figure 17: Carving including an image of tusk-like teeth.

Figure 18: Carving showing tusk-like teeth similar to those in Figure 17.

strange. **Figure 21** shows a similar "jaguar". But since when have jaguars had snakes on their backs and the talons of a bird of prey? The image of this monster reminds me of those cargo cults that claim that ritualistic honouring of technology, such as airports and airplanes, will bring with it material wealth (cargo) [2]. The depictions are finely chiselled representations, as if cut into the granite using a

Figure 19: Carving of a figure holding a rounded object in its fist.

Figure 20: Carving conventionally held to depict a jaguar.

Figure 21: Another supposed jaguar carving.

dentist's drill. **Figure 22** shows two winged "cherubim", a masterpiece of craftsmanship, cleanly engraved out of the panel. In all, as a local archaeologist told me, there were once 14 of these flying beings depicted at the site. Seven had looked north, and seven south. Today only fragments of these images remain recognizable.

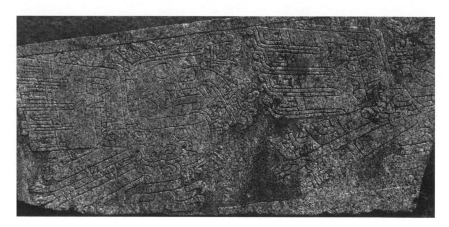

Figure 22: Carving of two winged creatures.

At the heart of one of the underground intersections stands El Lanzón **(Figure 23)**, the spectacular carved stele whose name means the "lance" or "spear". El Lanzón is almost 4m (12ft) high. However, the corridors around it are only about 1m (3ft) wide and 2m (6ft) high. The stele, which is twice as high as the tunnels, could not have been manoeuvred around any of the underground corners. It's clear that the planners of Chavín de Huántar must have maintained an opening in the ceiling from the very beginning of its construction in order to drop El Lanzón onto the crossroads inside the temple interior at a later stage.

Figure 23: El Lanzón

Figures 24–27: Stone heads at Chavín de Huántar.

The carvings on El Lanzón are just as obscure as all the other sculptural work we have been considering. And the stone heads **(Figures 24–27)** that protrude from the walls of the tunnels are equally inexplicable. We have no idea who these skulls are supposed to represent.

And things get even weirder. In the open air of the Sunken Square, one of Julio Tello's colleagues found an obelisk that today stands in the Archaeological Museum of Lima. Known as the Tello Obelisk **(Figures 28–33)**, it has baffled even the most knowledgeable Peruvian archaeologists since its discovery – and it is still waiting to be deciphered. Like hundreds of other onlookers, I have stood uncomprehendingly in front of it, photographing the object from every angle, hoping for enlightenment – but nothing.

Figures 28–30: Tello Obelisk

And there is more. The least comprehensible of all the mystifying artefacts from Chavín de Huántar is the Raimondi Stele. Peruvian geographer and scientist Antonio Raimondi (1826–1890) found this wonder in the centre of the Chavín de Huántar complex and had it transported to Lima in 1873. When it comes to inscrutability, this spectacular incised granite slab breaks every record.

Figures 31–33: Tello Obelisk

Figures 34–35: Raimondi Stele

Fashioned out of black diorite, the Raimondi Stele is 1.75m (almost 6ft) high, 73cm (2¹/₂ft) wide and 17cm (7in) thick. On the Mohs scale of mineral hardness (with 1 being the softest and 10 the hardest), diorite has a rating of 8 – only diamonds can cut into it. The delicacy of the engravings **(Figures 34–35)** testifies to an inconceivable precision, to the use of jigs and rotating drills. With all that in mind, what does academic opinion say about the Raimondi Stele? Here's a snapshot:

Professor Dr Miloslav Stingl [3]:

"The Raimondi Stele represents the Jaguar Man. From out of his godlike head more and more highly stylized Jaguar men are growing ..."

Dr H.D. Disselhoff [4]:

"... an upright Jaguar Man, holding in each hand a multifaceted sceptre richly decorated with curves. The lower part ends in stylized heads of beasts of prey, and the upper part a plant-based emblem ...."

Dr Rudolf Pörtner and Dr Nigel Davies [5]:

"... represents a figure with the head of a beast of prey. Both of its hands, pointing out at right-angles, hold a decorated rod, which extends far beyond the head of the figure ... Headdress with mouths layered one on top of the other and tongues hanging out ... and snake heads ...."

Professor Hermann Trimborn [6]:

"... shows in flat relief a feline monster with sceptres in its claws. It is crowned by a whole structure made from the yawning maws of beasts of prey, from which serpents emanate."

Professor Horst Nachtigall [7]:

"An half-animal half-human standing figure is depicted, with an animal head and a decorative headdress

*consisting of monster heads, framed by a glowing halo.
Hands and feet show animal claws; a snake-belt encircles
the body."*

Professor Dr Siegfried Huber [8]:

*"The details of the relief carving are like codes: fangs,
snake heads, puzzling interlacing, eyes – symbolic
without explanation – surreal, if any word at all can
fit with it. A petrified threatening gesture of a fear-
filled existence."*

Dr Friedrich Katz [9]:

*"Here too we can find hair in the form of snakes and
facial features which are strongly reminiscent of a
jaguar. The Raimondi Stone is made up of a
stratification of several bodies and faces in an almost
hideous form."*

Dr H.G. Franz [10]:

*"In the standing figure, the cult leader, priest and
shaman is depicted with a mask, which appears as a face
mask or a masking shawl made of animal pelts in a
fantastical re-formation ...."*

Dr Inge von Wedemeyer [11]:

*"... the consummate image of the highest incarnation of
the godhead, the creator god Viracocha."*

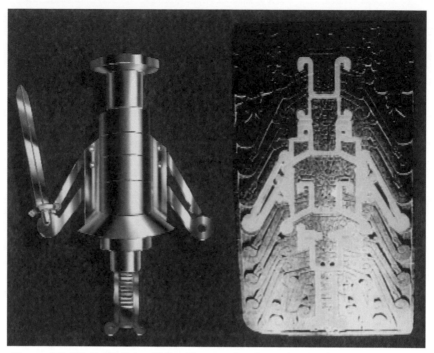

Figures 36–37: Dr Wolfgang Volkrodt's reconstructions of technology depicted in the carvings on the Raimondi Stele.

That's a real mishmash of interpretations from the experts! Every one of them can see something different. Which interpretation do we believe? The highly stylized Jaguar man? Plant-like emblems? Mouths with tongues hanging out? A monster with sceptres? Maws of beasts of prey? A monster head with decorative headdress? A fear-filled existence? Hair in snake form? A cult leader wearing a mask? Animal pelts? The creator god Viracocha?

As with so much that concerns the old world, these interpretations of the Raimondi Stele have a whiff of misunderstood technology. Perhaps it's less a question of "Jaguar men", "highly stylized heads", "masks piled high" or "sceptres", and more of a motor powered by a steam engine, a highly technical, multi-functional machine …

This idea is not as audacious as it sounds. Dr Wolfgang Volkrodt, a brilliant German engineer without any archaeological preconceptions, has interpreted every detail of the carvings on the Raimondi Stele as pure technology [12]. By the simple act of viewing the stele upside down, the correlations become obvious: he has identified a steam-producing boiler with latched retaining springs, injection nozzles, snap levers, rotary pistons, air ducts, leaf springs and ball joints **(Figures 36–37)**. It's a convincing technological interpretation that makes sense of every detail on the Raimondi Stele, leaving nothing out.

So what was the purpose of this machine? Volkrodt believes it must have been used to hoist, cut and transport heavy loads. The question is how these ancient people, the builders of Chavín de Huántar, would have picked up the technical knowledge required to construct such a machine. Or, to turn it around: *who sent them* this carefully constructed multi-function steam engine, and who instructed them in its usage?

More questions: who gave the Ark of the Covenant to the prophet Moses in the Bible? Who gave the biblical Noah the exact dimensions for building an ark? Who destroyed the enemies of the Pharaoh with a winged sun-disc coming out of the sky? [13] Who carried our ancestor Abraham into the cosmos? [14] In which workshop did the "flying machines", known as *vimanas*, originate in ancient India? [15] Who were the "Watchers of the Heavens" in the book of the prophet Enoch? Who was his teacher in astronomy? [16] And so it goes on. Ancient texts abound with descendants of mysterious heavenly instructors.

The very existence of Chavín de Huántar continues to mystify the experts. The site has no precedent and its development is impossible to position on the established human timeline. This problem has become apparent to archaeologists. Professor Dr Miloslav Stingl, a member of the Czech Academy of Sciences, says:

> *"The appearance of Chavín culture resembles rather an explosion, an unexpected discharge, the effects and consequences of which are in fact dispersed right across Peru."* [3]

From Dr H.D. Disselhoff, an expert in Peruvian art, history and culture, we have:

> *"It's my conviction that a still unexplained influence from the outside contributed to the development of Chavín culture."* [4]

This is exactly the point made by German ethnologist Professor Walter Krickeberg (1885–1962):

"It has often been pointed out that the development of higher culture in ancient America did not take place ... in slow, continuous steps, but in leaps and bounds, you could almost say explosively ... the oldest American high cultures appear on the scene without any advance notice: this includes, in the Andean countries, those of Chavín. This remarkable phenomenon can only then be satisfactorily explained if you assume that there were one or several impulses, which have acted upon the old America from the outside." [17]

And this is how it is. Chavín de Huántar did not experience any slow-moving evolutionary development. Let's think about this. People cleared and levelled off 50,000 square metres (538,000 square feet) of uneven, rocky terrain in the high mountains. A deep-lying drainage system was designed in such a way that the later, upper buildings fitted exactly to the underground infrastructure. Expert knowledge was needed of advanced stone-working tools and of how to transport the blocks over mountainous terrain. There were artists on hand with the ability to engrave, with incredible precision, innumerable granite and diorite plates. The Raimondi Stele proves that they must have used diamond drills to achieve this. What kind of team could do this? And what do those engravings really depict? The hybrid animal–humans they often show could just as easily be seen as robots. Did the artists have any idea what they were portraying and were they acting out of some notions of tradition or did a mighty, unknown power tell them what to do? And why do the whole thing in the first place?

Ancient texts from all cultures describe events that could never have actually happened. In the Bible, for example, the prophet Elijah flies up to heaven with fiery horses. Our ancient ancestors knew that a horse can no more fly than spit fire. In the same way, there were no flying jaguars, let alone flying snakes (which the Maya speak of). In the Sumerian–Babylonian poem the *Epic of Gilgamesh*, the heroes Gilgamesh and Enkidu hurl bolts toward a monster:

"Chumumba himself saw them coming. He had paws like a lion, his body was covered with bronze scales, on his feet were the claws of a vulture, and the horns of the wild beast were on his head .... They shot the arrows at him, threw their projectiles. The missiles bounced back, and he remained unharmed."[18]

In the Old Testament (Book of Job, 41ff.), the prophet Job describes a fire-breathing Leviathan that has variously been interpreted as a whale or a crocodile:

"His bones are as strong pieces of brass, his skeleton like iron bars ... out of his mouth go burning torches and sparks of fire leap out. Smoke goes out of his nostrils as out of a seething pot. His breath scorches like glowing coals .... When he raises himself up, the mighty are afraid, and they become mad with terror. Before his teeth

a sword cannot be held, nor spear, nor missile or yet armour ...." [19]

Such a creature has never existed at any point in history. I suggest that this example, and every similar one from the ancient texts, actually describes a misunderstood technology (just like a cargo cult) – nothing more than that. And what the scriptures describe in words, the carvings describe in pictures. The Raimondi Stele of Chavín de Huántar depicts technology. Where, then, did it come from?

In my work *History is Wrong!*, I looked at the Book of Mormon [20]. I highlighted an underground metal library mentioned there, which does in fact exist in Ecuador. Although the Book of Mormon is a religious and not a scientific work, it contains parts of a real history that date back thousands of years, just as the Bible and the Torah do. The written testimony in the Book of Mormon may very well describe the origins of Chavín de Huántar, with its incomprehensible technology and enigmatic engravings. In order to clarify these connections, I need to introduce you to some of my thoughts from *History is Wrong!* [20]

In the Book of Mormon, the bible for the Mormon faith, a tribal chieftain by the name of Lehi becomes witness to a heavenly descent.

"And it came to pass as he prayed unto the Lord, there came a pillar of fire and dwelt upon a rock before him .... And it came to pass that he saw One descending out of the midst of heaven, and he beheld that his lustre was above that of the sun at noon-day." (Book of Mormon, 1:6ff.)

The same thing happened with other major figures in the ancient texts – Moses [19], Abraham [14], the Pharaohs [13], Enoch [16], Arjuna [21]. In the Book of Mormon, it's Lehi [22].

The being that emerges from the pillar of fire orders Lehi to summon his tribe to travel to a remote land. Under the guidance of the mysterious Lord, the clan builds eight ships. The "Lord" then hands over 16 glowing "stones" – two for each ship – to illuminate the ships' interiors. In addition, Lehi receives eight compasses, one to steer each ship. To state it in plain terms: Lehi and his clan were not engaging with a supernatural god who could produce wonders out of nothing. A god of wonders wouldn't have required lights or compasses; in fact, wouldn't have required ships at all. If they had, they would have been built according to the principles of engineering, not (as described) "after the manner of men".

Mormon researchers are convinced that Lehi's crew put to sea off the coast of today's Gulf of Aden and reached the South American coast via the southern Pacific Ocean. [23] Lehi was a Jaredite – a descendant of Jared, the sixth patriarch before the Flood. After the elderly Lehi had passed away, his son Nephi took over command. His successors call themselves Nephites, but the entire people, with its many branches, still calls itself Jaredite. And what did Nephi do in that strange mountainous country that we now call South America?

"And I, Nephi, did build a temple; and I did construct it after the manner of the temple of Solomon save it were

*not built of so many precious things; for they were not to
be found upon the land, wherefore, it could not be built
like unto Solomon's temple. But the manner of the
construction was like unto the temple of Solomon; and
the workmanship thereof was exceedingly fine."*
(Book of Mormon, Second Book of Nephi, 5:16)

So, according to this statement, a temple was built in South America
on a smaller scale than the one that Solomon created in Jerusalem
in ancient times. It was laid out taking into account the four cardinal
directions. It comprised a complex of outer and inner courtyards, a
main temple containing many corridors and rooms, a sanctuary and
perhaps something "mysterious", similar to the Ark of the Covenant.
In addition, there was a water channel and four gates that pointed
in the four cardinal directions. Finally, the structure was somehow
connected to the sacred number seven. Last but not least, the temple
in South America was built out of nowhere, so to speak, without any
precedents in the typical South American cultures of the time.

There is a long tradition associated with the number seven. Among the
Jews, the seven days of creation, like their seven-armed candlestick (the
Mehorah), testify to this. The Revelation of St John speaks of the Book of
Seven Seals. Seven also plays a similar role at Chavín de Huántar. There
are fourteen – two times seven – "cherubim" engraved on the monolithic
plate over the main gate. Seven of them looked toward the north, and
seven toward the south. Further down on the Sunken Square, where
archaeologists found the Tello Obelisk, stands the Altar of the Seven

Goats. This is also known as the Altar of Orion, because seven holes in the altar plate roughly show the seven main stars in the constellation of the same name. The Raimondi Stele depicts seven "arms" or "snakes" on each side. In fact, researchers have discovered that the number seven is represented everywhere in the temple at the site [24].

The similarities between the complex at Chavín de Huántar and King Solomon's Temple in Jerusalem do not stop at the numerous references to the sacred number seven:
* Both sites are aligned along the four cardinal directions.
* Both are shrines, religious centres and places of pilgrimage.
* Both temples stand above subterranean tunnels and canals.
* Both are made up of three terraces, one on top of the other.
* Chavín de Huántar contains a ventilation system in its windowless sanctuary and artificially lit inner chambers – so does the Holy of Holies in the Temple of Solomon in Jerusalem.

And there are other similarities to bear in mind:
* The leaders or the priests at Chavín de Huántar had received technologies from their God that were ahead of their time – as did Moses, Solomon and others in the Old Testament.
* The builders of Chavín de Huántar worshipped a flying god – as did the Israelites.

This last statement will provoke the counterargument that the Israelites had worshipped only the one ineffable God. But it was the God of Israel, who descended in fire, tumult, earthquake and smoke, as the Old Testament so impressively portrays:

"And Mount Sinai was altogether on a smoke, because the Lord descended upon it in fire: and the smoke thereof ascended as the smoke of a furnace, and the whole mount quaked greatly." (Exodus, 19:18)

And what was it that Lehi witnessed in the Book of Mormon? The Lord stepping out from a pillar of fire …

Ultimately, of course, there remains the important Commandment to make no image of God for yourself: "Thou shalt not make unto thee any graven image, or likeness of any thing that is in heaven above…." (Exodus, 20:4). As a result there could be no representation of God in the Temple of Solomon. Nor is there one in the complex of Chavín de Huántar – only difficult-to-understand abstractions.

Let's consider what this all means. What could have induced a group of people in that far-flung era to travel from Israel to distant South America? Why should the Nephites construct a building "like unto Solomon's Temple"? What sense is there in all this?

Thousands of years ago a group of alien ethnologists landed on Earth. Some of those extraterrestrials (ETs) mutinied against their leader and started having sex with the daughters of humans. You can read about this in the Bible, where these outsiders are called "fallen angels" or the "sons of God" (Genesis 6:1ff.). This is confirmed in detail in the Book of Enoch (6:1–5). The mutineers – not exactly tactful when it came to their methods – all wanted to be served. They needed minerals, ores (including gold), food and so on. Our ancestors gave them their labour, assuming in their ignorance that the ETs were gods. The mutineers had no advanced weapons at their disposal, all of which had remained on board the mother ship. But each of these "fallen angels" possessed a knowledge that was centuries in advance of that of humanity. For example, each of them knew how to make a manoeuvrable hot-air balloon, as described in the Kebra Negast ("Glory of the Kings"), the book of the Kings of the Ethiopians [25]. Each of the mutineers knew what ingredients were needed to make explosives or for constructing a laser. They knew how to mix hard metal alloys, and how to build a primitive steam engine. They used this knowledge to impress the people and make them submissive.

As a result of their exploratory flights, one of these pseudo-gods knew of a distant continent, which was later to become South America. He or she directed a group of people there and told them to take their old scriptures with them – these scriptures, which arrived in the form of tablets, are what now forms the Book of Mormon. The "fallen angel", whom the earth-dwellers respectfully address as Lord, ordered the construction of a building similar to the Temple of Solomon. In the dungeons of the new buildings, the builders were to hide the tablets of scripture, consciously placing them so that, at some time in the future, someone might unearth them again. In order to give future peoples a clue as to their existence and to preserve them, the building was constructed of indestructible material and decorated with "cherubim" (flying beings). The hard diorite was to be inscribed with the enigmatic, technical messages that appear on the Raimondi Stele. The alien Lord was very well acquainted with the functioning of the human brain – he knew that our curiosity would get the better of us!

But why did it have to be so complicated? [20] Couldn't the alien Lord have communicated to the people of that time what was happening? But that would not have been possible. They would not have been able to communicate technological concepts to our prehistoric ancestors. Equally, the ET would have been aware that the old traditions would be distorted through religious interpretation over the course of millennia. They would also know that it was necessary for the people of the future to stumble across this enigma of a building in the high Andes, and that their curiosity would not give them peace until they had settled every question. The remnants of this logic are what are addressing us. The Lord even dictated to the servant Nephi:

> *"And blessed be he that shall bring this thing to light; for it shall be brought out of darkness unto light … yea, it shall be brought out of the earth, and it shall shine forth out of darkness, and come unto the knowledge of the people … and no one can prevent it …."*
>
> (Book of Mormon, 8:14ff.)

This goes for the information encoded in the Chavín de Huántar complex, and in the Metal Library in Ecuador [20] and in the Great Pyramid [26]. It's time to tackle the old matters with modern eyes. Then from nonsense suddenly comes sense.

In South America there are yet two more curious locations that we can link, at least culturally, to Chavín de Iluántar. First, is the Archaeological Park of San Agustín in the department of Huila in Colombia. As early as 1911, the Heidelberg professor Karl Theodor Stöpel (1862–1940) had penetrated underground chambers that no one seems to talk about today [27]. One year later, his countryman Theodor Preuss examined the huge stone sarcophagi there and ended up shaking his head, "because I have never found the slightest trace of a skeleton in them". The head-shaking continues even today. What was the purpose of these underground rooms with mighty sarcophagi in granite, if there is nothing in them?

Figures 38–40: Sculptures in the Archaeological Park of San Agustín, Colombia.

At San Agustín can be found the so-called "Forest of Statues" – 39 stone sculptures. No one knows who – or what – they are supposed to represent **(Figures 38–40)**. As you look at the images, consider their oversized canine teeth, just like those beings depicted in the carvings of Chavín de Huántar.

The San Agustín site also contains *La Fuente de Lavapatas*, the Fountain of Foot Washing, which appears to be a labyrinth of canals, basins, watercourses, rectangular pools and roundels on various levels **(Figures 41–42)**. On the rocks and the edges of the basins nestle reliefs of lizards, salamanders and ape-like animals. Tour guides explain that the whole scene depicts a woman giving birth. I looked at the chaotic scene from every angle, but I could not recognize anywhere a woman giving birth. What happens, though,

Figures 41–42: The Fountain of Foot Washing, San Agustín.

if we consider the mesh of basins and canals from a technical angle? Could they in fact represent a complex for the purification of metals? Perhaps liquid hot metal flowed from basin to basin, so that heavier components would sink to the bottom, lighter ones would be borne further along, with the impure elements and the dross remaining in the filters of the roundels and snaking troughs. The Inca, as well as the peoples before them, had incredible knowledge of alloys. Their smelting methods, casting techniques and plating procedures produced finished objects that looked as if they were made of pure gold – even though in reality gold made up only a micrometre-thin layer of each [29]. My suggestion for a metal-processing plant is just as reasonable or unreasonable as the idea of a childbearing woman.

Interestingly, the Fountain of Foot Washing has a counterpart approximately 2,800km (1,740 miles) away as the crow flies. At El Fuerte in Bolivia, near the village of Samaipata, is a hand-carved mountain peak. On top of the artificially flattened plateau lies a network of rectangles, roundels, basins and connecting lines **(Figures 43–45)**. There is, however, a significant difference to the river-fed fountain in San Agustín: El Fuerte is situated on the highest point of the mountain – there are no natural watercourses. This makes the concept of a fertility cult nonsensical.

Figures 43–45: El Fuerte ceremonial site, Bolivia.

Figures 46–47: Parallel grooves at El Fuerte.

Furthermore, El Fuerte is the only site in the world where two parallel, perfectly straight grooves, 38cm wide and 27m long (about 1¼ft by 81ft), run up a mountainside **(Figures 46–48)**. Is this a ramp directed toward the heavens? On both sides and in the centres of these artificially created channels are zigzag lines, with an unknown meaning. At the upper end of the ramp, cut into the rock, are circular roundels with triangular protrusions in a kind of catapult arrangement.

Figure 48: Parallel grooves at El Fuerte.

Figure 49: Model of possible interaction of a flying vehicle with the grooves at El Fuerte.

All this considered, could the following offer a viable explanation? Imagine that at the lower end of the ramp sits an anchored model aeroplane, a kind of toy aeroplane. A rubber band runs from the plane in between the grooves up to the roundel at the top. Strong arms stretch the rubber band and anchor it by means of beams in the triangular protrusions of the roundel. At a command, a priest breaks the anchoring, and the model rushes skyward **(Figure 49)**. Today's aircraft carriers are equipped with similar devices; and the tribes of South America were familiar with rubber before the Europeans.

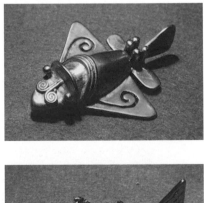

But what did these ancient peoples know of model aircraft? In fact, apparent sculptures of aircraft have been found in the tombs of the wealthy indigenous nobility of Colombia **(Figures 50–53)**. They cannot be meant to depict insects –

Figures 50–51: Colombian sculpture depicting flying machines.

they are, without exception, gilded, and seem to stand for what's valuable and what's divine. And flight tests, conducted from 1997 by Peter Belting, Dr Algund Eenboom and Conrad Lübbers, have confirmed that the models could actually fly. [30] What more evidence could you ask for?

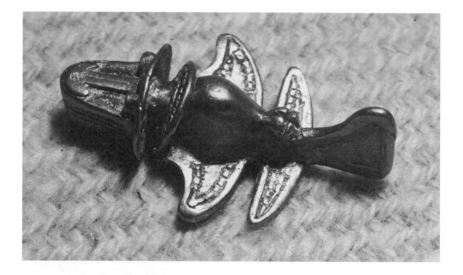

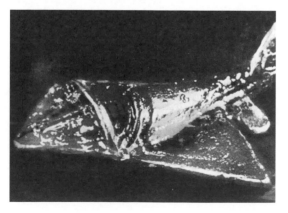

Figures 52–53: Colombian sculpture depicting flying machines.

CHAPTER TWO:

Divine Stonemasons

In the 16th century when the first Europeans stood before the vast, enigmatic ruins of the highlands of Peru and Bolivia, they wondered how it could be possible that human hands had transported and cut the gigantic blocks needed to build those monuments. The feat still amazes us. Scattered all around the Peruvian countryside are platforms put up by people whose history and origin we know nothing about, and of whose religion just a few legends remain.

In 1533, Spaniard Francisco Pizarro (c.1476–1541) managed to conquer the Inca capital Cuzco in Peru with a force of just 250 men. How was that victory over a well-equipped army of native troops possible? Pizarro was a special breed of villain: he had captured the supreme ruler of the Inca, Atahualpa, and presented him as a hostage. The battle-hardened Inca, far greater in number than the Spanish, seemed paralysed as Pizarro's men ransacked Cuzco. The Spanish demolished temples and, in their desire for gold and silver, melted down untold numbers of cultural treasures.

Located in the Peruvian Andes, Cuzco (from the Quechua for "navel of the world") lies 3,416m (about 11,200ft) above sea level and about 350km (215 miles) northward of the incredible Lake Titicaca (the highest navigable lake in the world) across the border in neighbouring Bolivia. According to legend, Manco Cápac, a son of the sun-god Inti, and his sister Mama Ocllo, landed from the heavens on the Island of the Sun in Lake Titicaca. Their father handed a shining staff over to the siblings and entrusted them to establish a settlement where the staff sank in the ground. And so it happened: at the point in the landscape where two rivers converged, Manco Cápac placed his staff and founded Cuzco. [31, 32]

Francisco Pizarro had no idea that the city was said to have been founded by a son of the sun god. He respected neither priest nor temple, nor did he hear the lamentations of the people of Cuzco, nor their cries of pain, when his men stormed the most important temple of the Inca Empire, Coricancha – the temple of the sun god in Cuzco. Spanish chroniclers reported that the preserved mummies of the Inca rulers were found sitting on Coricancha's golden thrones, that all the rooms held tapestries of silver and gold, and that a mighty golden sun-disc and many stars had blazed from the ceiling. The Spanish conquistadors brutally destroyed the altars to the gods, tore down multicoloured painted ceilings and melted down the great gold and silver showpieces.

They left the astonishingly cleanly arranged stones intact, and used them as the plinth for their Church and Convent of Santo Domingo. The 6m (18ft) wide curved wall at the west end of the convent even survived the earthquake of 1950 **(Figure 54)**. While many modern

Figure 54: Church and Convent of Santo Domingo, built over the Inca Coricancha.

buildings in Cuzco fell down after various earthquakes hit the city, most of these ancient Inca walls remained intact. However, the church of Santo Domingo didn't come away from the 1950 earthquake completely unscathed. Cracks appeared in the church floor, bringing to light polished blocks.

Just below the current main altar of the church is a small hole, which is an entrance into the subterranean world of the *chinkana*, the Quechua word meaning labyrinth. This labyrinth is made from galleries and tunnels cut from the rock, which intersect, wind and bend over and under each other, running in all directions. Few feel

Figures 55–56: Inca stonemasonry inside the labyrinth below Cuzco.

comfortable in these claustrophobic underground vaults. The Spanish chronicler Garcilaso de la Vega (*c*.1501–1536) dared to venture only as far in as the daylight penetrated. Considering the tools the Incas had at their disposal, this incredible subterranean network demonstrates an inconceivable masterpiece of stonemasonry **(Figures 55–56)**. The precise work is a feast for the eyes – except that no one can figure out the purpose of all that polished stone. The block shown in Figures 55 and 56 reminds me instinctively of the door to a modern bank vault.

A gold plate, engraved in 1613 by a direct descendant of the Incas, is said to represent the cosmological conception of the sun-god Inti and his children. Beside the sun, groups of stars, a cross formed by stars and what we presume are planets, there are two human figures. Are they Manco Cápac and Mama Ocllo **(Figure 57)**?

Figure 57: Gold plate, perhaps engraved with images of Manco Cápac and Mama Ocllo.

Figure 58: The *Hiram Bingham* train to Machu Picchu, Peru.

Approximately 75km (about 47 miles) northwest of Cuzco lies the world-famous ruined city Machu Picchu, nowadays flooded with tourists. A practicable road link between the two locations is under construction, while the Inca Trail, the old Inca path, and a phenomenal railway also link them. Only 30 years ago, the railway was serviced by a rickety old train. You half expected the rattling carriages to jump right off the tracks, and pigs and turkeys charged around among the passengers on the train. Today, the transport is rather more luxurious. Every train includes a dining car serving delicious Peruvian delicacies, and a bar with live music. Hiram Bingham, the name of the reputed discoverer of Machu Picchu **(Figures 58–59)**, shines in gold lettering on the wagons – but more of that later. The route is operated by Orient-Express Hotels & Train Cruises, just as if the travellers were journeying between Paris and

Figure 59: Entertainment on board the *Hiram Bingham*

Figure 60: Railway tracks leading up to Aguas Calientes.

Istanbul. Modernized train or not, it still takes four hours to cover the distance from Cuzco to Aguas Calientes, the village at the foot of Machu Picchu **(Figure 60)**. On the way, the views of the Urubamba Valley are breathtaking. Then, 60km (37 miles) from Cuzco, at an altitude of 2,792m (9,160ft), the enigmatic ruins of Ollantaytambo reveal themselves before the passengers' eyes. Its sun temple was supposedly built by the pre-Inca creator god Viracocha [33]. We have

Figures 61–62: Wall of the
Six Monoliths, Ollantaytambo.

only to look at the Wall of the Six Monoliths **(Figures 61–62)** to understand the high standard of work and cunning construction methods Viracocha must have insisted upon.

Figure 64: Hiram Bingham Highway zigzagging up to Machu Picchu.

Figure 63: The station at Aguas Calientes.

Aguas Calientes, the terminus station for Machu Picchu, lies in a curve of the Urubamba **(Figure 63)**. From there, an unpaved, zigzag road, known as the Hiram Bingham Highway, leads up the steep stretch to Machu Picchu **(Figure 64)** itself. It's said that US explorer Hiram Bingham (1875–1956) first discovered this ancient city in 1911. But, while he can lay claim to having been the first to make its existence widely known to the public, in fact the locals knew about it long before he got there. And if we start looking at European explorers, Bingham's claim is weaker than ever: as early as 1865 the Italian Antonio Raimondi (see page 33) had published a map mentioning Machu Picchu by name; and in 1874 the German land surveyor Herman Göhring plotted Machu Picchu on a map (albeit not in the correct place).

And there are more. In 1894 Don Luis Bejar, a German adventurer came to the ruins – but a young man called Augustín Lizárraga had shown him the location. And it was Augustín Lizárraga who led Bingham to Machu Picchu 17 years later.

As an aside, Luis Bejar and Augustín Lizárraga together discovered an ancient temple along the side of the Urubamba riverbed. They concealed the exact location because of the treasures they found lying there. In 1930 Oswaldo Paez Patino, an engineer working on the railway line, uncovered the entrance. Together with Oswald Patino, the then Peruvian Deputy José Pancorbo ventured into the underground galleries and then gave instructions to conceal the entrance from view with the aim of making it impossible to find again.

Figure 65: Visitors marvel at the spectacular ruins of Machu Picchu.

Figures 66–67: Terraces at Machu Picchu.

No one knows the true origins of Machu Picchu, but its beauty is beyond description **(Figure 65)**. The French sociologist and philosopher Roger Caillois (1913–1978), a member of the Académie Francaise, called it "a hymn in stone of lavish, even shocking magnificence". [34] It is the most inaccessible of all the Inca fortified towns, their strongroom. Today, many archaeologists assume that an Inca ruler, wanting to hide away from the marauding Spanish conquistadors, ordered its construction as his place of retreat, hidden high in the Andes. But in fact this Inca city existed long before the Spanish ever drew near.

The word *machu* means "old" and *picchu* means "summit". Machu Picchu, therefore, is an "old summit". A second peak, the Huayna Picchu, rises up directly opposite, making the two look like oversized sugar loaves. Right down in the depths of the valley runs the silver ribbon of the river, the rumble of which you can hear in Machu Picchu itself. The first builders, who created terraces on what is a dangerous precipice, cannot have been ancient people. Why not?

This is the jungle and it rains on Machu Picchu for days on end. When that happens, small rivulets start forming, which go on to join together, forming larger streams that hurtle down into the valley, dragging off everything that lies in their path. After two summers of weather like this, ordinary terraces would normally have been washed away. But some of these seem literally to stick to the steeply

Figures 68–69: Classic Inca walls at Machu Picchu built of rounded-edge stone blocks.

sloping cliff faces **(Figures 66–67)**. The civil engineers who built them, thousands of years ago, knew how to prevent any collapse. They did not simply clear the ground to construct each terrace, but put down a layer of crushed, water-permeable stones along the entire length of each one. They installed wastewater ducts, which channelled the overflowing water down into the Urubamba River. Subsequently, they levelled off several larger flat areas on the rocks and built 290 buildings on top of them. This miracle of engineering is so intelligently constructed that it remains concealed from the Urubamba Valley below.

The chronicles of the Spanish conquistadors tell us that the soldier Miguel Rufino saved an Inca maiden from rape, but in the process

killed his fellow soldier with his sword [35]. After that he decided to lay low with the Inca woman, and they marched for several days along winding pathways finally arriving at a holy city. Rufino describes this city as having a meandering river far below and two mountain peaks. His account is so exhaustive and accurate that there can be no doubt he was in Machu Picchu. On arrival, the hero and his beloved swore to obey the laws of the Inti, and never to betray to a stranger anything about the location. They were allowed to take refuge there, in a dilapidated palace within the city walls, which became their home for a year. The story seems to show that, by the time of the Spanish, at least some of the buildings were unused or ruined, which means that Machu Picchu can't have been built as a fortified place of refuge during the Spanish conquests.

There are three different architectural styles at Machu Picchu. First, there are the low walls and smaller agricultural terraces, like those that indigenous Andean peoples continue to use today for farming. Then, there are the classic Inca walls with their square and rectangular stones rounded off at the edges (Figures 68–70). There are often transverse beams, put there by more contemporary restorers, resting on top of these, with fill material heaped on top.

Figure 70: Classic Inca walls at Machu Picchu built of rounded-edge stone blocks.

Typical trapezoidal openings appear everywhere **(Figure 71)**. Finally, there are gigantic megaliths, often hundreds of tons in weight, on which everything else rests **(Figures 72–78)**.

Figure 71: A typical trapezoidal wall opening.

Figures 72–74: Examples of wall construction at Machu Picchu incorporating megaliths.

Figures 75–78: Examples of wall construction at Machu Picchu incorporating megaliths.

Figure 79: The Watchtower

The signs are that no single generation built Machu Picchu. The underground area is megalithic and existed a long time before any Inca ruler put up the walls. Cut granite runs laterally across the steep slope of the natural rock. It's clear that individual structures have been grouped around it, including the so-called Watchtower with a megalithic granite structure on its floor **(Figure 79)**. To this day no one knows what this structure was actually for.

Furthermore, the building now called the Royal Mausoleum clearly shows styles from two different eras – megalithic and Inca **(Figure 80)**. It is cut out of the natural granite, and the seven steps leading down to the mausoleum itself are made from one piece of rock, in contrast to every other example of Inca style, which uses smaller stones, rather than megalithic ones.

Figure 80: The Royal Mausoleum

The Intihuatana (meaning "hitching post of the sun"), also known as the Sun Stone, stands at the highest point of Machu Picchu. In order to construct this monument, the builders would have had to plane down a large piece of natural rock to create a flat surface (leaving the "hitching post" protruding), and then carved the resulting block in several places, creating different levels, gradients and angles **(Figures 81–83)**. Each of the monument's four sides is aligned to one of the four mountain peaks that surround Machu Picchu, and the sculpture finishes in a highly individual upright spur that extends its flattened-

Figures 81–83: The Intihuatana

off finger up to the sky. A diagonal extended from one corner of the flattened surface to the diagonally opposite corner points precisely toward a small stone window on the upper edge of Huayna Picchu, the hilltop standing opposite. The sun rises at that exact spot at the vernal and autumnal equinoxes, when day and night are of equal lengths, each year.

The only certainty about the provenance of Machu Picchu is that we are all – scientists, archaeologists, me – beginning with many assumptions. I have trouble imagining an Inca tribe building Machu Picchu on those steep slopes merely at the whim of their ruler. Where is their incredible technology in such a theory? Before the engineers chipped the first terrace out of the solid rock, they knew how to control the problem of water washing away their work. They also understood how to cut granite to give smooth surfaces, and how

Figures 84–86: Tilting, polished rock faces at Q'inque Grande, Peru.

to transport blocks weighing several tons up the steep slope of the mountainside. The Spanish chronicler Cristóbal de Molina (1529–1585) tells us that the sons of gods such as Inti and Viracocha instructed humankind in how to cut stone and in astronomy [32]. Later, however, the people disappointed the gods and their sons. Why? Because they started to worship god figurines – effigies of gods, rather than the gods themselves. The parallels with God being angry with Moses (and others) are unmistakable. The Inca gods withdrew, leaving the Inca people anxiously scanning the heavens, registering every change, every movement on the horizon, around the clock, looking for signs that the celestial beings would return. The notion of the return of gods or a God appears in all religions around the world.

Machu Picchu's megalithic construction style is just as obvious as it is in Cuzco. In the region of Cuzco, the archaeological site of the Q'inqu Grande lies just a few metres from Sacsayhuamán, the Inca citadel found on the road toward Pisac. It's an inexplicable stone structure attributed to Viracocha, the creator god. In Quechua, *q'inqu* means "full of twists", and that exactly describes the citadel. Rock faces more than 3m (12ft) high tilt slightly forward and are

Figures 87–90: Steps, niches, corners and roundels carved into the rock at Q'inqu Grande.

polished smooth **(Figures 84–86)**. Above them are inexplicable steps, niches, corners and roundels cut out of the rock **(Figures 87–90)**. Between them are clefts in the rock with walls, small shelves and gradations carved into them **(Figures 91–92)**.

Figure 91: Carved rock face at Q'inque Grande.

Figure 92: A shelf carved into the rock at Q'inqu Grande.

Figure 93: Stone workings near Sacsayhuamán.

However, I think, in its original form, the Q'inqu Grande must have been quite different from how it looks today. I suggest that every tourist turns their back to the Inca citadel at Sacsayhuamán and instead pokes about in the countryside behind it. It is full of fissured but clearly worked rocks that are still in good condition. Above ravines and caves are colossal blocks, precisely chiselled out of the rock. Smoothed and polished walls **(Figure 93)** make no sense at all in their present positions, with apparent entrances to caves or tunnels being interrupted, terminated or running into each other, moved out of their previously straight courses **(Figure 94)**. Even the notion that the whole thing had once been a quarry does not hold together, because the carved walls are often situated only a few centimetres away from worked block next to them. A stonemason

Figure 94: Stone workings near Sacsayhuamán.

Figure 95: Worked rock faces sited close together, near Sacsayhuamán.

working here would not even have had the room to swing an arm to wield a tool **(Figure 95)**. Nothing is coordinated here with anything else, there is no element that holds the picture together. The edges run razor-sharp and perpendicular. And behind every bend, new absurdities await.

Figure 96: Smoothed surfaces lead to natural rock, near Sacsayhuamán.

These are megalithic riddles for which there is no obvious answer. There is no overall scheme that would make sense of these strange walls and rock projections. Surfaces as smooth as concrete end in the natural rock **(Figure 96)**. And stairways have been built upside down along the ceiling **(Figures 97–98)**. But who could possibly have run up those?

Figures 97–98: Staircases run upside down along the ceiling!

Low Inca walls around these enigmatic rock masses have led archaeologists to describe the site as an Inca cult location. They describe platforms as "sacrificial altars", chiselled-out sections are designated "Inca thrones", and every recess becomes evidence of a "death cult". However, we actually know nothing at all about these rock workings. The complex was constructed using techniques that we do not understand, at a time long before our own, and by beings

Figure 99: Glacial erosion, slipping in different directions, has revealed evidence of stonework lying beneath.

unknown to us. Even the glacial erosion visible on the mountainside leads only to uncertainties **(Figure 99)**. Normally, glaciers would slide down a mountain slope toward the valley, but that's not the case above Cuzco. Here, they ran in different directions. What's more, remnants of stone-working can be found even underneath the glacial erosion. So what came first? The glacier or the wall?

Figure 100: The concentric stone circles at Muyuq Marka, Peru.

Above Sacsayhuamán lies Muyuq Marka, a structure made up of several stone circles that is commonly referred to as an Inca calendar. The best way to view Muyuq Marka is from an elevated position. The stone circles are divided up by "spokes" – there are monolithic blocks, hewn out of andesite, dividing the site into smaller chambers **(Figure 100)**. All this spontaneously reminds me of sites in China. But what should China have to do with South America?

The Inca rulers regarded themselves as "sons of the sun", as descendants of heaven. The same is true of the Chinese emperors. The primordial rulers of China (and Tibet) are said to have descended down from the sky on flying dragons [36]. The "sons of the sun" in Peru did so using solar barques. All the descendants of those heavenly sons, whether in China or the Andes, saw themselves as divine beings. In China, for centuries the rulers regarded themselves as the representatives of the highest of civilizations. They believed they had originally received their teachings, their technologies and their astronomical knowledge directly from their heavenly fathers. In the 11th century BCE, the Zhou dynasty defeated the last ruler of the Shang, potentially ending the cult of the "heavenly ones". But in fact that's when it really began. The Zhou rulers lived according to the rules of Tianming, the Mandate of Heaven. *Tian* is the Mandarin Chinese word for the heavens, the concept of which was firmly established throughout Chinese culture. Every ruler was called Tianzi, the son of heaven. Regents who did not live and reign in the spirit of Tianming could not be real sons of the heavens and were deposed or killed. Is it any wonder, then, that all the Chinese emperors had to undertake certain ceremonies and speak with their

Figure 101: The Altar of Heaven at Xian, China.

heavenly relatives on an "Altar of Heaven"? This is just like the South American sons of the sun. In China there are still two places that are called "Altars of Heaven". These are round structures divided by radial walls into different chambers. The Altar of Heaven in the Chinese city of Xian **(Figure 101)** could just as easily be transposed above the Inca fortress of Sacsayhuamán in Peru. The images are the same – and so are the traditions.

No one doubts that Sacsayhuamán **(Figure 102)** once bristled with weapons – but what was the citadel intended to defend? Certainly

Figure 102: The citadel of Sacsayhuamán.

not the city of Cuzco, which lies a long way below and is open and vulnerable from all sides. In fact, it appears there was nothing to defend at the Inca fortress; and it hasn't been built at any politically strategic point in the country's terrain. Unless, though, it was intended to defend the most important of all the sacred places: the Altar of Heaven.

CHAPTER THREE:

Legendary Times

In February 1968 my book *Chariots of the Gods* came out. Since then a new and alternative approach to the prehistory of our civilization has enriched the perspective of millions of people. Today, about 200 books exist worldwide invariably dealing with this one question: did our ancestors receive visitors from other parts of the cosmos? Ninety per cent of all the authors – whether they are scientists or researchers without an academic title – have arrived at the same answer: yes, our good old Earth has been visited by ETs.

Only established so-called "science" turns its back on the notion of extraterrestrial visitation. So often my conversations with scientists lead me to believe that there are few scientists who have any idea of the depth and scope of the evidence that exists to point toward ET intervention. The scientific world is one of order, of the explicable – and the notion of aliens is unsettling.

Across all editions, in 32 languages, I have sold more than 65 million copies of *Chariots of the Gods*. In the USA, since 2010, the History Channel has been broadcasting a TV series called *Ancient Aliens*. Now showing worldwide, it is the most successful TV series the

History Channel has ever produced. The series covers the same question as those many books: did our ancestors receive visitors from other parts of the cosmos?

So, what does all this have to do with the subject of my research? It's an echo. I get mail from all over the world, and am always meeting wonderful people who confide in me their discoveries. Some of these are holders of university professorships – they are themselves "official scientists", but they want to remain anonymous. In their letters and correspondence, they send me highly interesting and neatly documented dissertations, asking me to raise the topic of alien visitation wherever possible, but without naming them as research source and revealing their identities. What are they afraid of?

The answer to that is simple. They are afraid of losing their credibility, of being subjected to professional and public ridicule. We live in a world of free speech, meaning that it's easy for anyone to respond to anything personally, offensively or derisively, largely without censor; sometimes it's the political or religious comment that can be the most derisive of all, especially when confronted with evidence that forces us to think outside of the accepted norms or religious dogma. As a result I respect my champions' anonymity and am grateful for their support.

As Shakespeare wisely maintained, there are more things in heaven and on Earth than are dreamed of in our philosophy. Some of these things have to do with ETs, with technologies that are buzzing around somewhere out there and sometimes appear on Earth, or with past cultures that definitely existed but that don't break through into scientific thinking. Except they do in this book.

Did the lost city of Atlantis ever exist? Of course it did! The literature on the existence of Atlantis now covers some 20,000 volumes, and the overwhelming majority of Atlantis researchers agree that it did. The sunken island, first described by Plato [37], has been investigated in all its aspects [38, 39, 40, 41]. Were there – long before Atlantis – other continents with cultures, such as Mu (in the Pacific), Lemuria

Figure 103: Underwater wheel tracks at Cádiz, Spain.

Figure 104: Underwater wheel tracks on Malta.

(also in the Pacific) and Kásskara (in North America) that are also now lost? Obviously, there were. Scientists such as the Austrian geologist Heinrich Kruparz document it in illuminating fashion [42, 43], and the traditions of the Hopi Indians in Arizona confirm the former existence of Kásskara, a sunken continent in the area covered today by the Pacific Ocean [44].

There are increasing numbers of discoveries being made under the water. So many that even the greatest sceptics are left with no choice but to admit that there is something wrong with history as we've been told it. So many incredible manmade structures lie under the water. There's something resembling an underwater harbour at Lixus (Morocco) [45]; underwater wheel tracks at Cádiz (Spain), and on Malta **(Figures 103–104)**; stone circles on the seabed by the small island of Er Lanic (Brittany, France); underwater structures at Nan Madol in the Pacific **(Figures 105–106)** [46] and in Yonaguni (Japan)

Figures 105–106:
Partially submerged
structures at the
Pacific site of
Nan Madol.

Figures 107–108:
Underwater
structures at
Yonaguni, Japan.

(Figures 107–108). Recently, assiduous Google Earth explorers have discovered more and more straight lines under water. For example, on the Pacific Ocean bed are continuations of the famous lines in the Peruvian Nazca area. Every new discovery, whether in the Mediterranean, Atlantic or Pacific [47], provides us with fresh insight that we simply cannot ignore.

On 21 June 1999, a farmer from the village of Chandar, in Goa, India, showed Alexander Chuvyrov, professor of mathematics and physics at the State University of Ufa in Russia, a stone tablet covered in strange carvings. Chuvyrov had been looking specifically for tablets just like this one, as for centuries local traditions had spoken about curious stones that had been scattered around the village and its surroundings. The scholar, standing for the first time in front of one of these stones, named it the Daschka Stone, after his granddaughter who had been born that very day. The fragment is 1.48m (4½ft) long, 1.06m (3ft) wide, 16cm (6in) thick and weighs about 1 ton. As Grazyna Fosar and Franz Bludorf write [48], the scientists from various disciplines who have since studied the Daschka Stone were confronted with a puzzle. The "stone" is

constructed of three superimposed layers: 14cm (5½in) dolomite is followed by 2cm (¾in) diopside glass and then 2mm (⅛in) calcium porcelain. The upper two layers must have been artificially applied. Engraved into the diopside glass layer are markings that to date have never been successfully translated, but represent a kind of three-dimensional map. During an online conference held on 6 June 2002, Professor Chuvyrov said that the Daschka Stone was in fact only a fraction of a larger slab, the other parts of which still remain to be found. Grazyna Fosar and Franz Bludorf report that the layer of diopside glass was applied using a technique that still eludes us [48]: "The actual relief has been worked into this glass layer. Over that there is a white layer of calcium porcelain that is barely

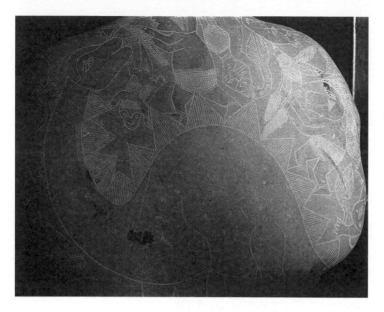

Figure 109–111: Cabrera Stones, Peru.

two millimetres thick, which seems intended apparently to make the delicate surface resistant to any blows or shocks." How old is this anachronistic artefact? Supposedly tens of millions of years. It fits into evolution like a Black Forest gateau in a Mars crater.

I have written before about engraved stones of a different kind [49]. Those found in the home of the Cabrera family in Ica, Peru, are, like the Daschka Stone, hundreds of thousands of years old. There have been continual attempts to undermine my research into the validity of the famous Cabrera Stones. The farmer Basilo Uschuya, who initially found many of the stones, has been accused of being a forger. Various people claim to have made the discovery of "forgery", but in fact I was the first person to explain Uschuya's work [50], I myself witnessed Uschuya making some engravings on the stones! The truth of it is that, as well as Uschuya's engravings, there are genuine, ancient marks on the stones – a fact that several geologists' support [49]. Some of the Cabrera Stones are now

located in a small museum in Lima that belongs to the Peruvian Air Force and is closed to the public. On these stones can clearly be seen millennia-old engravings that show objects flying across the skies, as well as engravings that depict people with beings that look like dinosaurs (**Figures 109–111**) – although, of course, in the accepted course of history humans and dinosaurs could never have encountered one another.

What other evidence in stone is out there for such an encounter? My critics know nothing about the prehistoric, inscribed stones of Glozel (France), the human–dinosaur figurines of Acambaro (Mexico), the human–dinosaur representations and the unknown scripts in the Crespi Collection (Cuenca, Ecuador), the human–dinosaur footprints found in the same geological layer beside the Paluxy River at Glen Rose in Texas, USA **(Figures 112–113)**. Palaeontologists have struggled with this discovery in Texas [51]. The well-meaning cheerleaders for evolution do not waste their time reading the books of US writers and creation researchers Michael Cremo and Richard

Figures 112–113: Human and dinosaur footprints at Glen Rose, Texas.

Thompson [52]. Correspondingly, they cannot know anything of the metal balls, each of them millions of years old, found around the mining facilities in the western Transvaal near the town of Ottosdal in South Africa. Today, there are a few of them in the Klerksdorp Museum, some showing three closely lined parallel grooves around their middles, and none coming from any particular culture that we can identify [52]. Nor can they know anything about the geode that was found on 13 February 1961 on the edge of the Amargosa Desert (California) that housed a metal pin in its interior [46]

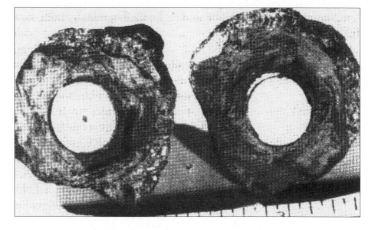

Figure 114: Geode found in the Amargosa Desert, California.

(**Figures 114–115**). The existence of the pin in an object that is at least 500,000 years old provides evidence of significant knowledge of metallurgy at that time. If we allow our only point of scientific reference to be evolution, we miss all these details and the alternative explanations they provide for us.

Barely 80km (50 miles) northeast of Lima is the Andean plateau of Marcahuasi in Huarochiri province, Peru. It's a four-hour drive from Lima to the village of San Pedro de Casta, then a further journey on foot or horseback to Marcahuasi, at an altitude of 3,963m (11,890ft). Only a few decades ago, hardly anyone was interested in visiting Marcahuasi, but now, between April and October, about 5,000 tourists a year scrabble around the dry and rocky area. So, why is it suddenly so popular?

The place is eerie. Esoterically inclined people speak of a very strong, inescapable energy field. Above, on the plateau, visitors clamber over the collapsed walls of a 13th-century culture. However,

Figure 115: The Amargosa Geode with the pin it contained.

according to Dr Daniel Ruzo, a lawyer from Lima, the original Marcahuasi must be hundreds of thousands of years old. He has spent months looking around Marcahuasi with a camera and a tape measure [53]. Depending on the light and the time of year, among the rocks you can see figures from an unknown world. There are heads emerging as if they had been hammered out of the rock long before the flood. There's a formation that the local people call the Monument of Humanity. By daylight, you can make out 14 different faces that blend into each other according to the position of the sun. By night two sphinx-like figures appear, each looking imperiously across the levelled area as if through a veil of time. At every turn you feel as if you are being watched, as if the priests and gods from a sunken world are everywhere.

Why should people from a long-past culture have sculpted heads and faces into the natural rock formations? Probably for the same reason that we too place monuments in the landscape. In South Dakota, USA, southwest of Rapid City, is Mount Rushmore. With jackhammers and tons of dynamite, the faces of US presidents George Washington, Thomas Jefferson, Theodore Roosevelt and Abraham Lincoln were smashed and blasted out of the bare rock there. Close by, a mountain massif has been modelled into a gigantic statue of the Native American chief Sitting Bull on horseback. Today, these magnificent rock monuments are carefully tended, and kept free from grass and bushes. But what will people say many centuries from now, when only fragments of the presidents' faces are still recognizable? Will they classify the four heads and the equestrian statue as the "geological whims" of nature? They probably will, because ultimately rational people would never have reshaped whole rock faces into monuments.

And as with the inscrutable rock formations above Cuzco, visitors to Marcahuasi find themselves standing before stone boulders that surely did not assume their present form by any natural means. So, when, how and by whom were they shaped? The inhabitants of San Pedro de Casta will testify that Marcahuasi is also a location for UFO sightings. Almost every resident will claim to have seen UFOs here. Unidentified flying objects are as natural in Marcahuasi as the cows that graze there.

The same applies to the mysterious plateau of El Enladrillado in Chile – in the province of Talca, about 60km (37 miles) east of the small town of the same name. There, too, UFO sightings are part of the everyday life of the local population; and their town also lays claim to a completely unknown technology. Why do UFOs visit the remains of long-gone cultures? Do those who use them know how to travel through time? Humberto Sarnataro Bounaud, who headed an expedition to El Enladrillado, noted, "Without doubt, a bygone culture has lived in this place. The natives of this area would never have been capable of building anything like this." [54] A few years ago Chilean teacher Rafael Videla Eissmann studied El Enladrillado and wrote a carefully documented booklet on the riddle of this high plateau [55]. In a conversation with me, Eissmann asserted, "Something here does not add up. No peoples have lived here for thousands of years. Our Chilean archaeology would know this. These cut blocks must come from an ancient culture." **(Figure 116)**

Figure 116: Cut stone blocks at El Endladrillado, Chile.

From what kind of culture? Surely there could not have been anything similar that existed before our present technological age. Otherwise, these beyond-ancient forbears of ours would definitely have left us some written testimony of their existence. Surely we would have found traces of them everywhere; those unknowns would have tapped our deposits of raw material on Earth long ago.

Figure 117: Tunjo Stones Archaeological Park, Colombia.

There's an archaeological park containing the Tunjo Stones located about 40km (25 miles) from Facatativa, in Colombia. Even the Colombian archaeologists do not know what these stones (*piedras*) are actually for. Engravings, reminiscent of chemical formulae, appear on some of the blocks. Scattered around the park are square and rectangular blocks of stone that look like gigantic friezes or ceilings that must once have rested on strong columns and then collapsed thousands of years ago. Even as a non-geologist, I know that nature creates amazing wonders that can look like polished monoliths or artificial rock walls, but the evidence of the Tunjo Stones is irrefutable. Even the passage of hundreds of thousands of years, and a vast array of potential interventions from nature itself, cannot create perfectly straight lines that run around whole blocks in a regular rectangle **(Figure 117)**. If these massive stone blocks had crashed down from the mountain, we might then have a possible explanation. But you can look far and wide and find no fractured cliff faces. The suggestion that the original inhabitants must have regarded the area as a holy sanctuary is backed up by these strange geometrical incisions and by the existence, not too far away, of the Leyna Stones.

These form a rectangle of monoliths, as found also in Europe and in North Africa, for example at Mzora, Morocco. As if to demonstrate that the thinking of the ancient peoples of the world was in accord, the rectangle at Leyna is neatly aligned astronomically according to the four cardinal directions – just like the megalithic standing stones at the Cromlech of Crucuno in Brittany, France. Today, in Leyna, there are 24 menhirs along the rectangle's longer side; in Brittany there are 22. The rectangle of Leyna must originally have consisted of 76 menhirs, plus a few columns up to 6.4m (19ft) high. These are now lying on the ground in the middle of the rectangular area **(Figures 118–119)**, while a few stone phalluses lie on the ground barely 1km (½ mile) away. The experts say it's a fertility cult, but for me that explanation is far too neat.

We are prisoners of our thinking system, of relying upon evolution to explain everything. In our pursuit of scientific order, we ignore verifiable facts – or we remain unaware of them in the first place. In one of the bays of Lake Titicaca, on the Bolivian side, Austrian explorer and engineer Arthur Posnansky (1873–1946) stumbled

Figure 118–119: Leyna Stones, Colombia.

across an old building with 3.5m (10½ft) thick walls. The Bolivian newspaper *El Diario* wrote on 14 July 1931:

"It is known that the Earth passed through several ice ages, during which vast lakes and meltwater developed, and these once covered the Bolivian highlands … this building must have originated before the Ice Age, when Lake Titicaca was not as large as it is today." [my emphasis]

Professor Dr Edmund Kiß, who had carried out excavations for many years in the highlands of Bolivia, wrote:

"That (the ruin of) Tiahuanaco once stood completely under water is certain. The large freestanding staircase is covered by a thin layer of lime that's been deposited by the water, and it's so firmly fixed that it must be scraped with a knife to take a sample."

The present archaeology takes no account of the fact that the limestone deposits are still evident today. The same applies to the ceramics in a layer of sediment. Dr Kiß:

> *"The bones of humans and animals, including some now extinct animal species, are lying in a disorderly heap across miles and miles of the alluvial deposits at Tiahuanaco. At one point this bone sediment is about 3.5m (11½ft) thick …. Here the railway runs through a narrow cutting, and this has sides 3.5m (11½ft) high but this doesn't even reach the bone sediment. Beneath the rails there is still the same sediment, composed of millions and millions of lesser and greater bone fragments,* broken shards of glazed ceramics, malachite beads, and much more …."* [my emphasis]

To my friends who have a different way of thinking, ceramic is manmade. There are no ceramics without people, and yet here – once again – we find ceramic in sediment that is tens of thousands of years old. Nonetheless, sceptics want to uphold their need for order, and even if their approach is, in many cases, out-and-out unsubstantiated, it still gets labelled as "scientific".

In the Jungfrau Park in Interlaken, Switzerland, visitors can admire an impressive collection of meteorites, documented with the location where each one was found. Every one of the extraterrestrial objects, and there are more than a hundred, is genuine. And broken fragments keep appearing, which look as if they have been artificially worked somewhere in the universe. Dr Max Flindt, a physicist who worked for years alongside the developer of the US hydrogen bomb Dr Edward Teller, told me about a meteorite with an indisputably artificial hole. This hole had been bored into the meteorite and was not the outcome of any natural process. The meteorite itself was formed of a kind of steel alloy that is unknown to us. Space junk? Part of a rocket? Impossible. It was discovered on 26 April 1952 to the southwest of Olancha, California, at a time when no manmade satellites were orbiting the Earth. Max Flindt wrote:

"The find shows that a space ship exploded somewhere in the cosmos. Or the piece of steel came from a planet, which for its part scattered into pieces, and parts of it shot as meteorites into the cosmos." [57]

Also relevant to this chapter is a find that was reported by the German Press Agency in the summer of 1977. Three rusty-coloured discs, apparently made of metal, turned up in a coal mine in southern Australia. They had a diameter of about 1.5m (4½ft) and a thickness of 45cm (1½ft). The biologist Dr Mac Lawrie, who was the first to give the curious objects a superficial examination, said that he had never seen anything like them in his life. His colleague, Shirley Kempf, claimed:

"The discs could prove to be the greatest discovery of the century. They may be small scientific probes sent to Earth thousands of years ago by alien beings from their mothership." [58]

Newspapers also reported a local Aboriginal legend of a vehicle coming down from heaven countless generations ago [59]. But, what subsequently became of the discs? A good acquaintance of mine made a thorough pursuit of the matter from the mine to the Ministry of Science. He discovered that a US official removed the discs for analysis – since then they have disappeared.

Just as incomprehensible are the glazed stones that have been found at locations all over the world. US author David Hatcher Childress has reported on these several times [60]. For example, since 1932 curious finds of yellow-green glass have been made in the region of the Saad Plateau, at the Great Sand Sea that stretches between Egypt and Libya. They have become known as "Libyan desert glass", and the British magazine *New Scientist* wrote in July 1999 that up to that point more than 1,000 tons of the strange desert glass had appeared, with the largest single piece weighing 26kg (57lb). Researchers initially assumed that a meteorite impact must have produced the material, but there was no trace of a crater visible anywhere in the vicinity.

This riddle would have been solved if it could have been shown that, without impacting the Earth, a meteorite had released hot gases that swept across the area, creating the desert glass. But for this to have been the cause, the various locations of the desert glass would have to have lain more or less along a straight line. However, they did not. Instead, the deposits were located in an oval, oriented along an east–west axis, and covering an area of 130 by 53km (81 by 33 miles).

The glass is 97 per cent silicon and looks like a yellow–green precious stone. In an analysis published in the scientific journal *Nature*, naturalist Dr Spencer is quoted as saying, "It is easier to assume that the stuff just fell from the skies." [61] Glass fragments have also been discovered in Death Valley, California, in the area between the Gila and San Juan rivers; and in Pakistan, lying beneath the millennia-old ruins of Mohenjo-Daro.

In Patagonia, Argentina, we find a mystery of a different nature. There is an enigmatic national park, the Monumento Natural Bosques Petrificados de Santa Cruz, located in the Department of Deseado, south of Fitz Roy. In a national park you might expect to find beautiful landscapes, snowy mountains, blue lakes and bizarre rock formations. But there is nothing of the sort at the Bosques Petrificados ("petrified forest"). The landscape is dry, windstorms blow across the arid steppes, and you can go a long way without encountering any human habitation.

This is not a forest as we normally imagine it, but a landscape of tree trunks spread out across the terrain with pieces of bark and cones scattered on the ground – everything ossified. Experts estimate that the forest is at least 70 million years old. At that time there must have been a warm and humid climate prevailing in Patagonia. Then, when the Andes began to rise from out of the sea because of the oceanic plates pushing upward, the new mountains blocked the damp winds coming in from the Pacific. At the same time volcanoes began to erupt and they threw huge amounts of ash across the forests. This ash held back the process of decay in the dying trees, isolating the trunks from the air. That is why tree bark, knot-holes and even pine cones are still preserved today.

But how did the actual petrification come about? The rain of ash did not kill the roots in the soil. Instead, the continual rain washed the easily soluble silicate salts from the ash, draining them into the ground. There, the roots drank them up and then slowly released them to the fibres of the tree trunks. Over tens of thousands of years, cellulose within the trees turned into stone. The result is the stone forest stuck in time, along with all the semi-precious stones, so-called agates, that cover the whole area.

At least, that is the scientific explanation for the petrified trees. The length of the trunks can reach 50m (150ft). Their roots, which are up to 2.6m (8ft) wide, still lie in the ground. Some of the fragments remain a mystery. For example, some trunks have been cut into eight or twelve equally sized pieces **(Figure 120)**. They have been cut through the trunk, as if with a saw: there's not even the slightest fragmentation in the wood, and there's not a single branch left sticking out from any part of any trunk. Who could have used a saw tens of thousands – even millions – of years ago? No one. At least not according to our current model of evolution. It is interesting to consider this in the light of the following story from Egypt:

On 14 September 1988, a Romanian Egyptologist (who prefers to remain anonymous) wrote to me with a highly unbelievable story.

Figure 120: Sawn log at the Bosques Petrificados, Argentina.

I am telling it to you anyway, because I got to know the man personally at a later date and his integrity impressed me. The Egyptologist was, in the summer of 1986, part of a team involved in excavating part of the Valley of the Kings in Luxor, Egypt. He was employed by the Romanian University of Craiova (a city in the west of the Wallachian lowlands). At a depth of 10m (30ft) the archaeologists came upon an apparently insignificant grave. The walls bore no paintings or hieroglyphs. In the middle of the dark tomb stood a sealed sarcophagus, again without any paint on it, and it contained dried fruits, ceramic figurines of cats, toy figures carved out of ivory, and finally the bandages of a small mummy. Once the linen had been removed layer by layer, they revealed the body of an approximately six-year-old boy with a diagonal incision slanting across the thorax. In his chest was an artificial heart. The not-altogether-serious *Weekly World News* [62] later reported:

> *"The heart consisted of manmade material and*
> *unknown alloys. It is an artificial heart, smaller than*
> *our hearts and much more technologically advanced.*
> *Both the fixed and the mobile parts fit together in a way*
> *that is unfamiliar to us … The artificial heart had*
> *clearly been placed there surgically. The natural heart*
> *was missing. This heart transplant has been done in*
> *such a way that our surgery today has no knowledge of."*

The Egyptian journalist Ahmed El Mansour speculated in a daily newspaper in Cairo that either the heart had originated from an earlier, unknown culture or had been transplanted there by ETs.

What then has become of the corpse and the artificial heart? My Egyptologist said that two inspectors of the antiquities department had wrapped the mummy in plastic for the purposes of research, sucked the air out, and then carried the parcel away. Later he had learned that carbon-14 dating had concluded that the body was 5,000 years old. He never heard anything again about the mummy and the artificial heart. One employee at the Egyptian Museum, though, said that the whole affair did not concern the Romanians, nor the rest of the world. The whole subject needed to be dropped.

So as far as the story goes, and I pass it on with qualifications, 5,000 years ago someone had an interest in saving the life of a six-year-old boy. Was it that person's own child? At that time the Fourth Dynasty ruled in Egypt. These were the pyramid builders. As is known from the investigations into countless mummies, 3,000 years ago Egyptian surgeons were already amputating single toes and replacing them with pieces of wood: the occupant of tomb TT-95, for example, is a female mummy with a wooden big toe. Furthermore, ancient Egypt abounded with medicines and potions. The Ebers Papyrus alone, now kept at the University Library in Leipzig, contains 776 recipes for medicines for all sorts of aches and pains. The science of medicine was well developed, and there is no question that the doctors at the time were well-acquainted with the human organs, which were handled separately during mummification. But, in ancient Egypt, artificial materials and alloys unknown to us today did not exist.

The Africanist and scientist Dr Milan Kalous, who lectured for several years at the University of Maiduguri (Borno State, Nigeria), wrote to me about an equally impossible find. Through his work he came into contact with the legendary Sao Culture. The Sao lived around Lake Chad (in Africa) and have traditionally been regarded as a race of giants. Dr Kalous reported that the clay vessels of the Sao were so large that it was impossible to imagine normal-sized people creating them. Some of the vessels are 5m (15ft) high, with sides 10cm (25in) thick. Their ceramic figurines are also intriguing: "They are grotesque and fantastical and show mysterious creatures that cannot be classified as either human or animal." The key location for the Sao people is the village of Ndufu, which was said to have been a city in former times. There – according to local legend – people had once upon a time met with the "Heavenly Ones".

Dr Kalous wrote:

"What Herr von Däniken suspects took place in various high cultures really did happen in Ndufu. I have evidence for my conclusion. This is not based on the Sao Giants, but rather the realism of the Ndufu Terracottas. That is, they show details that would have been unimaginable to the people living by Lake Chad. These figures are sustained by a certain naturalism, which could best be described as 'plastic photography'. What the figures show is not some kind of African imaginative ability, but historical reality. The creatures are simply not of this world. We have here the first reliable images of extraterrestrial astronauts."[63]

So where is the photographic evidence? Dr Kalous told me that the figurines were in the possession of an old family, regarded as royalty by the tribe. They safeguard the figures as highly honoured ancestors and do not allow any photos. I only hope that someone younger than me might be able to pick up this trail at another time, gain the confidence of the king of Ndufu and see the figurines for themselves.

Curiosities? Absurdities? I've written in previous books that millennia ago a network of perfectly straight lines lay across Europe. These aren't lines that we can draw over the map and which by chance happen to cross some old ruins. Certain ancient tribes purposely constructed their first sanctuaries at designated points on the lines, and no one knows why. This network of lines spreads across the whole of Europe and it's hard to ignore. The lines extend over hills, mountains and valleys, linking prehistoric constructions as if they were set on a string of pearls. Even more so because the names of the linked sites themselves often carry the same etymological root origin (for example, Calais, Mont Alix, Mont Alet, L'Allet, Alaise, L'Allex, Alzano, Calesi, Cales).

The whole of ancient Greece lies beneath a geometric grid – it was put there long before those ingenious mathematicians Euclid, Plato or Pythagoras. Now, French filmmaker Patrice Pooyard points out in his movie *The Secret of the Pyramids* [64] that entire ancient cultures also run in straight lines across the globe: Paracas with its "Candelabra" (Peru); Nazca (its geoglyphs, Peru); Ollantaytambo (Peru); Machu Picchu (Peru); Sacsayhuamán (Peru); Mali (Dogon, Africa, Sirius Mystery); Tassili (Algeria, rock paintings of "astronauts"); Siwa (Oasis in Egypt, Oracle of Amun); Giza (pyramids, Egypt); Petra (Jordan, tomb of Aaron); Ur (Iraq, ancient kings); Persepolis (Iran, city of the gods); Mohenjo-Daro (Pakistan, glazed stones); Khajuraho (India, temple on top of older ruins); Pyay (Myanmar, pagodas on top of older ruins); Sukhothai (Thailand, temple on top of older ruins); Angkor Wat (Cambodia, temple on top of older ruins); Easter Island (Pacific, statues). I have traced the 40,000km (25,000-mile) line on a globe and found it to be essentially straight with a variation of around only 100km (60 miles).

In the 1970s, the Russian historian Nikolai Goncharov, working with scientists Vaelry Makarov and Vyacheslav Morozov, plotted the locations of the important sites of ancient cultures on a map of the world. Looking at this map, Goncharov saw that the positions of the sites together created the image of a ball with a crystalline structure. To quote from the *Komsomolskaya Pravda* [65]:

"Therefore, many of the centres of ancient cultures did not have random locations, but lay exactly at the nodal points of this system. Thus it was with the Indus culture of Mohenjo-Daro, with Egypt, with northern Mongolia, with Ireland, with Easter Island, with the Peruvian cultures and even with Kiev, the 'mother of all Russian cities'. Along the seams, where the gigantic 'plates' meet each other, extend the oil fields of North Africa and the Persian Gulf. The same thing can be observed in America from California to Texas. Of course, this sort of connection can't be noted in every single instance. And yes it does appear on several occasions that the phenomenon is purely coincidental. As for the rest, deviations from the geometrically strict scheme are completely understandable. The reason for this is that our planet does also change, and the creation of our natural resources does continue."

There were spooky aspects of this that no one had come across before. For example, the distance from Nazca in Peru to Giza in Egypt is the same as that from Teotihuacán in Mexico to Giza. Or:

Angkor Wat in Cambodia is the same distance from Nazca as Mohenjo-Daro is from Easter Island. Was there, all those many thousands of years ago (I really don't dare suggest any figures), something like a global construction commission? With designated areas where people had to settle? Did the oldest cultures originate in places that had a connection of some kind with energy or natural resources (petroleum, minerals, and so on)? Who told the people where to go? Why? And when did the horrific events, that today appear to us as fairy tales, actually take place? Does humanity have a mythical past? How old, in fact, is the human race? The answer to that particular question is not documented anywhere in history, but why? Because all the great libraries of the ancient world, consisting of more than two million books, were destroyed. This means that we can fill in the gaps in the mysterious past of humankind only through religious literature.

Followers of the Jain religion, in India, claim that the founding of their religion took place hundreds of thousands of years in the past, long before Buddhism. Their faith is eternal and unchanging. The Anuttaraupapātikadašāh tells the story of the earliest saints, who had ascended to the highest heavenly realms. In the Purvagata there are scientific teachings, such as the behaviour of substances (that is, what we call chemistry). The Twelve Upangas teach us all sorts of details about astronomy, but also about the life-forms resident in other solar systems. And the Kalpa Sutra provides information about the leaders of Jainism, the so-called Tirthankaras. In each Kalpa (that is, in each age or era), 24 Tirthankaras appear. The first of the

Tirthankaras was Rishabha. He walked the Earth 8.4 million years ago. The last two Tirthankaras died in around 500 and 750BCE respectively. Another, Arishtanemi, arrived on Earth about 84,000 years ago.

The Jains believe that their ancient scriptures were originally passed on from one generation of priests to another. For the Jains the loss of a script is not especially painful, because every Tirthankara possesses in his own memory the whole body of knowledge. The astounding thing with the Jains is the frankly incredible cycle of ages within which the past has played out and within which the future will play out. For the Jains, 8,400,000 years comprise a so-called Purvanga; 8,400,000 of these Purvangas correspond to a Purva. The Jains' counting system goes on to include 77-digit numbers.

The Jains' scriptures even describe different planets outside our solar system. The realms of the gods itself in heaven has a name. It's called Kalpa (the same word alternatively used to mean age or era). There are meant to be magnificent flying palaces there, mobile structures that are often the size of whole cities. Are what's described ships built to house whole generations? These celestial cities are arranged one above the other, so that from the centre of each floor, the smaller *vimanas* (sky chariots) can travel out in all directions.

Once an age expires and new Tirthankaras need to be born, a bell sounds in the main palace of the heaven of the gods. This bell causes a bell to start ringing in each one of the other 3,199,999 celestial palaces. Then the celestial ones gather together for talks. Some of them also visit our solar system in their flying palace. And on Earth begins a new age.

Is this all nonsense?

The ancient Babylonian royal list WB 444 gives ten primordial kings from the creation of the Earth to the Flood. They ruled for an amazing total of 456,000 years. After the Flood, "the royal family descended once again from heaven", and the 23 kings who followed ruled in total for another 24,500 years, three months, and three-and-a-half days. Egypt was no different. The priest Manetho reports that the first divine ruler in Egypt was Hephaistos, who also brought fire with him. There then followed Helios, Agathodaimon, Kronos, Osiris, Typhon, and Horus. Manetho tells us of names and data that archaeology cannot comprehend, but that nevertheless existed. A total of 380 kings are chronicled, who are nowhere to be found in official Egyptology [68]. The gods were said to have reigned over Egypt for 13,900 years, and the demigods and other dynasties that followed reigned for another 11,000 years. The historian Diodorus of Sicily (1st century CE) writes about these rulers in his 40-volume historical library (written some 2,500 years ago):

"From Osiris and Isis up until the reign of Alexander more than 10,000 years have flowed by, but some recount, that it might even have been just under 23,000 years." [69]

Are these all exaggerations? Around 700BCE the Greek writer Hesiod wrote down his myth about the five races of humans [70]. He tells us that the immortal gods – Kronos and his associates – created humanity. "That illustrious race of heroes, called the demigods, who in the time before us inhabited the infinite Earth."

Among the Mayan people in Central America there is a god named Bolon Yokte. As it said on a written tablet in Temple XIV at Palenque, this god was supposed to have appeared for the first time on 29 July 9,31,449BCE. And on the third tablet in the Temple of Inscriptions at Palenque, an inscription gives a date of 1,274,654 years in the past relating to the "Boy King Pakal". [71]

Madness? There is hardly any older culture on the face of the Earth – and I've studied so many of them – in which such statistics don't likewise appear, relating to events that never even get a mention in our historical accounts of prehistory. The ages of Buddhism are also immeasurably long. This is highlighted impressively in the Buddhist text called the Anguttara-Nikaya (Chapter IV) [72]. One Kali-Yuga lasts 432,000 years, a Deva-Yuga 288,000 years, a Treta-Yuga 216,000 years, and so on. The Kangyur, the sacred book of Tibet describes similarly lengthy reigns [73]. In the "Collection of the Six Voices" in the chapter "Divine Voice", we're told about the various heavens that exist on an exterior level. In the Heaven of the Four Great Kings, 50 Earth days correspond to one day and one night. One life span amounts to 500 years or, rendered in Earth years, nine million years. In the next heaven 100 Earth years correspond to one day and one night. One life span amounts to 1,000 years or 36 million human years. In the "Heaven of the Seven Treasures", the life span amounts to an entire 144 million years.

The problem with all these impossible numbers, which – strangely – occur all around the world, lies in evolution, which leaves no leeway for any cultures earlier than evolution's dawn. Twenty thousand years ago, our ancestors were painting their rocks; they lived in caves, gathered roots and berries, and the valiant menfolk joined forces for big-game hunting. That's it. Anything relating to a higher stage of development that might have existed hundreds of thousands of years or more ago has, according to Darwin's theory of evolution, to be nonsense. Within scientific circles, though, it is a sacrilege not to believe in evolution. Every person who doubts Darwin's teachings is considered ignorant. Meanwhile, hardly a year goes by without our being introduced at a press conference to yet another up-to-date discovery relating to the human species. Think of the times that a particular fossil has been considered the very latest definitive human ancestor, only to be usurped by another further down the line. The trajectory of evolution has not just been based on bone finds, but on DNA. But it's only the insider who discovers that the geneticists are supplying data that contradicts itself.

To formulate it clearly and unequivocally: of course we are products of evolution – but not of evolution alone. Right from the start – since the so-called "primordial soup" – there has been outside intervention, tangents of evolution and thought, even during this century, which has really barely begun. Evolution is indisputable. Even the Catholic Church, albeit after a delay of 120 years, has finally acknowledged Darwin's theory. In 1950 Pope Pius XII wrote in his encyclical *Humani Generis (On the Origin of Humanity)* that we should view Darwin's doctrine only as a hypothesis. The more open-minded Pope John Paul II, on the other hand, sent a message to the Pontifical Academy of Sciences in which it states, remarkably: "New discoveries make us see evolution as more than just a hypothesis." In a more qualified tone, the Pope states that the doctrine of evolution is valid just for the body: "The soul is created directly by God." [74]

The Secretary of the Swiss Bishops' Conference, Nicolas Betticher, has elaborated on this formulation:

> *"God took care of the Big Bang, He created stars, water, air and sun. This gave rise to the first cells, which went on to develop into amoebae, animals, and finally human beings. The difference between humans and animals is that God intervened in evolution, breathed His spirit into humanity, and created it according to His own image."* [75]

So God intervened in evolution, probably on a highly personal basis. The theologians of the Roman Catholic Church did not realize that with their new doctrine they destroyed the foundations of the Biblical creation story. What remains of the "Original Sin" if Darwin is right? And where is the need for "redemption" by the only born Son of God after an Original Sin that has never taken place? Incidentally, it was not God who created humans "in His own image" and who "intervened in evolution", but "the gods" – for the most part. In the original Hebrew version of the first book of Moses, the word *elohim* is a plural term. If you then replace "gods" with "extraterrestrials" that would be getting it about right.

However, it is unlikely that anyone will acknowledge this breakthrough until the ETs celebrate a festival in honour of endless creation in St Peter's Square, Vatican City, Italy. Then, the encyclical *Ad Honorem Extraterrestrium*, meaning "In Honour of the Aliens", will follow.

All this is absolutely not intended as blasphemy or based on atheism. Ultimately Creation will remain at the end of the chain as the cause of the universe. Or just, God. Even super-clever astrophysicists, who beyond the Big Bang do not know anything, make a claim for God or Creation being the start of everything. Something cannot come out of nothing – this is universally true, including in astrophysics.

Once again: life forms on this Earth have evolved according to the evolutionary model. But, before that, targeted and artificial mutations have come from outside. Our planet has never been a closed system. Brilliant scientists themselves have excellent arguments against the omnipotence of evolution. I would estimate that right now I have accumulated one hundred or so volumes of anti-evolution literature. There follow just ten names in chronological order, all top scientists, including biologists and anthropologists, who for 40 years have been fighting for a supplementary outlook upon evolution:

Teilhard de Chardin [76], Roland Puccetti [77], Max Flindt [78], Arthur Ernest Wilder-Smith [79], Fred Hoyle [80], Francis Crick [81], Bruno Vollmert [82], Arthur Horn [83], Michael Cremo [52] and Thomas Nagel [84].

The last of these, Thomas Nagel, studied at Cornell University (New York, USA), at Oxford in the UK, and at Harvard (Boston, USA), and is currently Professor of Philosophy at New York University. He is an internationally recognized scientist. Does this change anything? Since his latest publication, Professor Dr Thomas Nagel has endured a purgatory of criticism. His stubbornly Darwinist colleagues are indignant. What has this thoroughly honest scientist done wrong? He dared, with no equivocation, to call into question the Darwinian doctrine [85].

Today, we are seeing steadily fewer objective scientists than ever before – science has become partisan and scientists lack courage. And because we are so willing to easily accept the works of boastful, swaggering scientists, humanity ends up with an unscientific world-picture that nonetheless bears the label "thoroughly scientific".

If all there is is evolution, cultures such as Atlantis, Lemuria or Kásskara are impossible. The false labelling of evolution ideology prevents flexible thinking. Amen.

CHAPTER FOUR:

The Wisdom of the Kogi

On the Caribbean coast of Colombia lies the city of Santa Marta and directly behind it the Sierra Nevada de Santa Marta, the home of the indigenous peoples of the Arhuaco, the Wiwa and the Kogi. In the mountain range of the Sierra Nevada, with a highest point of 5,775m (17,300ft), there originate about 200 smallish streams, one of which is called the Buritaca. On both sides of this stream, which tumbles steeply down the mountainside, lies an old Kogi town called Buritaca 200 (the number 200 merely refers to the 200th stream), otherwise known as the Lost City. It is an awe-inspiring place, full of wonder.

During the last few decades, Buritaca 200 has been excavated under the direction of Dr Alvaro Soto from Bogota State University [86]. This city in the jungle of the Sierra Nevada is different from any other. A Colombian Air Force helicopter set me down on the top terrace of a platform, best described as being like the top tier of a wedding cake. The levelled terraces at the site interlock into and over each other, so that, in all, 32 larger and smaller surfaces stack up a height of 900–1,300m (2,700–3,900ft) **(Figures 121–123)**. Because of the complicated topography – rather like that of Machu Picchu in Peru

– the ancient builders had to flatten the terrain section by section, cutting away the steep slopes and filling and compacting the terraces with earth up against retaining walls (each between 60cm/2ft and 10m/30ft high), and then make them water permeable using pebbles and stones. None of these terraces has ended up being washed away. From the very beginning a drainage system was also integrated into the retaining walls, keeping the complex dry despite the constant

Figures 121–123: Buritaca 200, high in Colombia's Sierra Nevada.

humidity, and the characteristic torrential rainfall. The gigantic size of the site of Buritaca 200 leads us to conclude that there surely must have been a plan in place before all those masses of rock were removed.

At first I thought to myself that the top terrace had been formed more by chance as the result of an accumulation of stone slabs. But I was wrong. Buritaca 200 is a bizarre landscape of stone discs lying on top of each other; of curving walls, ellipses, small towers, staircases, and paths – all in an indescribable tangle **(Figures 124– 131)**. In whatever direction I looked, I kept seeing other platforms. Most of the time I was standing on an artificial surface, rarely on top of the natural soil. As I pushed through the undergrowth, I found yet

Figure 124: Terrace retaining walls at Buritaca 200.

Figures 125–127: Tangle of curving stonework at Buritaca 200.

Figures 128–131: The artificially created landscape of Buritaca 200.

Figure 132: The 1,358-step stairway at Buritaca 200.

more terraces, carefully built-up walls and steps. By one of these staircases I counted all the steps. There were 1,358 of them **(Figure 132)** – stone beam on top of stone beam. Professor Soto told me that archaeologists have discovered more than 200km (125 miles) of paths and roads of carefully placed stone. Waterfalls rush down the steep slopes and are skilfully intercepted and directed into a network of artificial canals.

Buritaca 200 is not a monolithic construction like Sacsayhuamán in Peru. Rather than 100-ton granite blocks, there are millions of stones and slabs of all different sizes **(Figures 133–136)** that have modified almost all the hillsides in the area. In the process, space was created for farmland, to provide food to feed a population of

Figure 133: Paving stones at Buritaca 200.

around 80,000 people (some 300,000 people are said to have lived in the entire Sierra Nevada de Santa Marta region during the pre-Colombian era). In the lowlands, indigenous peoples grew sugar cane, maize and tropical fruits of all kinds; and in the higher regions, onions, potatoes and various vegetables – many of which are still cultivated today.

Figures 134–135: Some of the huge numbers of stones used at Buritaca 200.

Spaniards Rodrigo de Bastidas (1445–1527) and Juan de la Cosa (1450–1510) explored the coastline of Venezuela in 1501 and pushed on towards Colombia to trade with the indigenous people there. Realizing that the locals were keen to offer gold items as part of their exchange, they gave them the misleading name Taironas, *tairo* more or less meaning "metal". However, the supposed Tairona Culture was actually the Kogi. For decades the Spaniards fought against them, driven by their greed for gold. They burned their villages, and kidnapped men and youths as slaves. The Kogi fought back with slingshots, wooden clubs and spears.

Figure 136: Stacked slabs at Buritca 200.

They also used poisoned arrows, extracting the poison from natural sources. Sometimes this came from the juice of the manchineel tree, a very toxic plant that resembles a pear tree but with fruit that looks similar to apples. The warriors coated their arrowheads in the juice, left them to dry, then wrapped them in palm leaves to protect themselves from the poison. The poison also came from an extract of the bark of the climbing vine *Strychnos toxifera*; this is known in modern medicine as curare and blocks the transmission of nerve reflexes to the muscles.

The war was a bloody one. The Spaniards lost about 3,000 troops, but the death toll for the Kogi was far higher, estimated to be 20,000 to 30,000. And all for a lust for gold. The jungle then became the realm of wildcats, howler monkeys, vultures and poisonous snakes. The primeval forest ate its way through the terraces and paths. The priests of the Kogi hid themselves among these barely accessible mountains of the Sierra Nevada, with thousands of their people. As a result, they survive today, preserving their customs and traditions, and the indigenous wisdom handed down from their forefathers.

The first person to study the Kogi scientifically and report back in detail was German ethnologist Professor Konrad Theodor Preuss (1869–1938). It was also he who had written already about the statues and underground installations at San Agustín (see page 50). Preuss found out that the Kogi derived their ancient laws from four original priests who had descended from the sky long before the Biblical Flood [87]. These original teachers had their homeland out in the cosmos, and every law reached the Kogi "from the outside". Each time these heavenly teachers came down to Earth, they wore masks. They could not reveal their faces.

This reminds me of the Babylonian "Epic of Gilgamesh", the first book of Moses, and the traditions of the indigenous Kayapo in the upper Amazon. In every case the indigenous peoples were not allowed to gaze upon the countenance of their respective gods. In the Gilgamesh story, "Whomever looks the gods right in the eye must pass away" [88, 89]. Moses never saw his Lord. And the heavenly instructor at the Kayapos showed himself in a closed-off suit without openings for the eyes, ears, nose and mouth [50]. The ET teachers must have been protecting themselves from the composition of Earth's atmosphere, and from the airborne bacteria in our environment, using masks and filters.

The Kogi priests handed down their holy office to their sons (just as with the Jains in India; see page 134). Today, that tradition still exists, each son entering a nine-year novitiate, during which he learns the knowledge of the fathers. That knowledge, therefore, passes down unaltered from one generation to the next. The priests are called *mamas*, and a *mama* is the absolute ruler. He can punish and praise without limits, because he knows himself to be in direct succession from the original cosmic priests. Today's *mamas* are also convinced that they stay connected to the cosmos through telepathic communication.

To achieve the degree of telepathy and hypersensitive spirituality needed to communicate with the heavens, the novices are locked up in total darkness for their nine-year induction. During this time they cannot work, or touch a woman, and they may eat only salt-free food. The Kogi priests also have a completely different sense of time to ours. They regard themselves as the "older brothers" and we are the "younger brothers". They speak of the Universe with an attitude of timelessness, as if it were all in the present, and of the Spanish conquests as if they had taken place only yesterday. Objects are not treated as inanimate or "dead" – everything is living. In various ceremonies, the Kogi, just like their brothers in the Arhuaco and the Wiwa, direct specific thoughts not only into natural products, such as roots, tree bark or foodstuffs, but also into stones.

Professor Preuss has transcribed the traditions of the Kogi:
> *Verse 1: "The mother of all our seed bore us in the*
> *beginning ... she is the mother of the Milky Way."*
> *Verse 12: "Thus the mother left behind a memento in all*
> *the temples. Together with her sons Sintana,*
> *Seizanhuan, Aluanuiko and Kultsavitabauya ...."*

Verse 38: "A thousand years then went past, and the world brought forth people with unnatural tendencies, the sort that would use all kinds of animals for sexual intercourse. The mother desired the son, the father the daughter, the brother the sister from the same blood ..."

Verse 39: "The son of Sintana saw this, and he opened the portals of heaven, that it might rain for four years ...."

Verse 40: "The priest Seizanhuan built a magic boat, and put all kinds of animals and others into it: All kinds of plants as well ... and locked the door."

Verse 41: "Now red and blue rain began to fall, and it lasted for four years, and, with the rain, lakes spread out all across the world."

Verse 43: "A total of nine years elapsed before all the lakes dried up, as the older brethren handed it down."

Verse 44: "Now all the wicked had perished, and the priests, the older brethren, all came down from heaven. Mulkueikai opened the door of the magic boat, and all the birds and four-footed animals went out. All the trees and plants began to grow. This was accomplished by people known as the Divine Fathers."

Verse 46: "And in all the temples they left behind a memento as a monument."

See how the texts resemble each other! The Kogi tradition speaks of bestiality – and a similar passage occurs in the Bible in Genesis,

Chapter 19, before the flood. In the Bible, God caused the Flood. Similarly, in the Jewish Book of Enoch the "Watchers of Heaven" are the cause [90]. With the Kogi it's the priest Seizahnhuan. In every case – and there are more – the flood is not a natural occurrence; something divine causes it.

"All came down from heaven", the Kogi tell us. Then, from a far-off location, the Sumerian–Babylonian Kings' list tells us, "After the flood, the monarchy descended once more from heaven." The Epic of Gilgamesh says the same. The similarities across these cultures, countries and writings are startling and undeniable.

For the Kogi the cosmos is defined as an egg-shaped space marked out by seven points: north, south, west, east, zenith, nadir (directly below the zenith) and midpoint **(Figure 137)**. Within the space are nine layers, or worlds, of which the middle – the fifth – represents our world **(Figure 138)**. Even today, the Kogi build their ceremonial houses according to this same pattern. So, the ground we walk on is the fifth layer, but above and below exist four more levels. The ceremonial houses also serve as calendars. In every Kogi village stands a large, round men's house (you can see an example of this in the Kogi settlement of Chivilongui), with a large stake protruding from the roof. The women's house stands diagonally opposite, and two crossed beams stick out from its roof-ridge. This women's house is located precisely, because at the vernal and autumnal equinoxes, the stake from the men's house throws a long shadow that then lies exactly between the shadows from the crossed beams of the women's

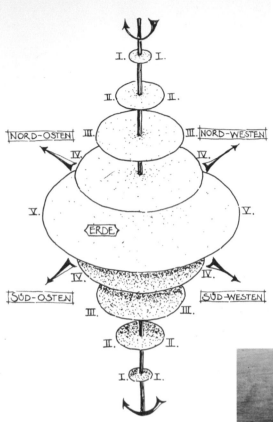

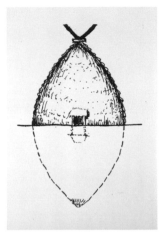

Figure 138: Kogi house embodying the egg-shape of the cosmos.

Figure 137: Kogi conception of a cosmos with layered worlds.

Figure 139: Traditional houses for Kogi women and men.

house (**Figure 139**). The phallus penetrates the vagina: a symbol of spring, of rebirth, when the seed must be placed in the Earth.

I know the different stories of the Great Flood, and I know that scientists have furnished evidence of several floods in several places around the world. But I also know the works of the old historians – Plato, Strabo, Diodorus, Herodotus, Enoch, Plutarch and so on – as well as the traditions of the Ethiopians, and of those in the Bible, the Book of Mormon, the Indian Mahabharata, the Mayan Popol Vuh, and so on. All these traditions, no matter where they originate, provide stories of a global flood, an annihilation of the human race and a new beginning. And in all the great myths and legends of humanity, the seed of life for the new beginning came from outside. This is true even of the Bible: "And God created man according to his own image, in the image of God created he him" (Genesis, 1:27).

So, evolution, yes, but before that information came from the Universe, and it did not occur by chance in the primordial soup [91]. Instead, an unknown extraterrestrial civilization, living on an unknown planet like Earth, released billions and billions of DNA particles into the atmosphere of the Universe. Those particles landed on Earth – a planet with similar conditions as their own home – beginning a new evolution, not by chance but by design.

CHAPTER FIVE:

Signs for the Celestial Ones

With the benefits of Google Earth, our landscape looks uncanny. If you thought it was only the Nazca peoples of Peru who had marked out gigantic images on the ground, looking on Google Earth you would soon know better.

In northeastern Jordan lies the area known as Harrat ash-Shaam. This can best be described as a dry wilderness in which animals have never grazed, water has never bubbled up and cities have never existed. There, of all places, at the ends of the Earth, around 1,000 strange circles are drawn on the ground **(Figure 140)**. They are made up of basalt stones pushed together in small heaps, each roughly

Figure 140: Stone circles of Harrat ash-Shaam, Jordan.

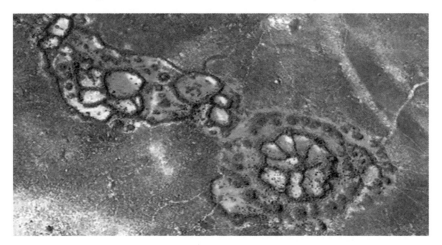

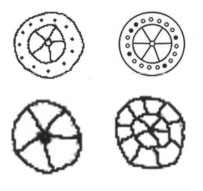

Figure 142: Earth drawing in the Atacama desert, Chile.

Figure 141: Differing formations of Jordan's stone circles.

5cm (2in) high, to create formations resembling wheels with spokes. More than 40 of these strange rings lie at the Azrag oasis, but the entire pattern is recognizable only from the air.

Furthermore, the circles appear at the ends of long, straight lines that, in turn, converge toward each other often over many hundreds of metres. Locally these depictions in the ground are called "kites" and the strange circles differ in shape and size. Sometimes they have a diameter of 3m (9ft), and at other times 9m (36ft). Sometimes spokes lead out from the centre to the rim of the wheel, and at other times the wheels are divided into different chambers **(Figure 141)**. Experts are inevitably reminded of similar depictions in Chile's Atacama desert (northwest of Antofagasta near the small town of San Pedro de Atacama; **Figures 142–143)**. The same motifs also exist in a reduced form in rock art around the world. For example, at Cete Cidades **(Figure 144)** in the northern Brazilian state of Piaui, and at

Figure 143: Earth drawing in the Atacama desert.

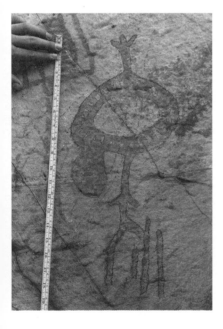

Figure 145: Rock art at Santa Barbara, California.

Figure 144: Rock art at Cete Cidades, Brazil.

Santa Barbara in California **(Figure 145)**. Or in a different form in Egypt, as a winged sun-disc. Professor David Kennedy from the University of Western Australia, who developed the project APAAME (Aerial Photographic Archive for Archaeology in the Middle East) in Jordan, together with his colleague Dr Robert Bewley, meanwhile speaks of 40,000 pictures visible from the air. Among them there are enormous images that are several hundred metres long **(Figure 146)**. Experts like Professor Kennedy estimate the age of these markings on the land to be between 5,000 and 7,000 years old. But the most important question still remains unanswered: who were the Stone Age desert dwellers making signs to?

Figure 146: Immense earth image, Jordan.

Lying on the ground 320km (200 miles) south of Tabuk, in Saudi Arabia, but near the Jordanian border, are some geometric figures up to 180m (540ft) long. They show pyramid-shaped triangles that end in a huge black ring **(Figure 147)**. The age of them is hard to determine, but they are certainly prehistoric.

Figure 147: Geometric figure at Tabuk, Saudi Arabia.

The spooky story continues. The oasis of Khaybar in Saudi Arabia, 150km (93 miles) north of Medina, is a thousand-year-old stopping-off place for caravans lying within the desert of Harrat Khaybar, which covers a surface area of about 12,000 square kilometres (4,630 square miles). This desolate region is renowned for several lava caves. Then, 100km (60 miles) northeast of Medina, aerial images identify more than 200 further kite motifs. In some of the grottoes in the area, archaeologists have found prehistoric rock drawings, bones and crockery. The creators of the drawings and crockery must also have been the creators of the rings and kites –

who else could it have been? And why did people thousands of years ago go to the trouble of fashioning immense signs in these searingly hot locations that are decipherable only from the air?

In addition to the kite motifs, Professor Kennedy has located rectangular lines that run parallel to each other in the area of Al-Hayt. They point in various cardinal directions and are several kilometres long. Again, hundreds of formations, looking like oversized keyholes, emerge one next to the other.

In an analysis of satellite surveys of the area around the Aral Sea (actually a landlocked body of water between Kazakhstan and Uzbekistan), Russian geologists have made a sensational discovery. From Cape Duan to the interior of the arid peninsula of Ustyurt, they found remarkable triangular formations on the ground. In an almost uninterrupted chain, gigantic triangles, with sides up to 1.5km (almost 1 mile) long, appear across several hundred kilometres **(Figure 148)**. The Uzbek archaeologist Vsevolod Jagodin, head of the Department of Archaeology of the Uzbek Academy of Sciences, said:

> *"The usual methods of archaeological investigation of the area are unsuitable in this case. The gigantic dimensions of the outlines make them completely incomprehensible to human proportions. Their reliefs are so smooth that you can travel a few hundred times along the individual sections without knowing that there is a unique archaeological monument under your feet."* [92]

Figure 148: Triangular formation near the Aral Sea.

The largest and most consistently recurring figures in these remarkable land drawings resemble huge bags with pillars attached forming a pyramid shape. At the top of each triangle is a ring about 10m (30ft) in diameter. The magazine *Soviet Culture* noted:

> *"Up to this point the system has been investigated up to a length of 100 kilometres. Scholars are convinced that it continues further and passes through the territory of Kazakhstan, and that, at its fullest extent, it surpasses the world-renowned system of mysterious lines and drawings in the Nazca Desert in Peru."* [92]

Professor Rolf Ulbrich from the Free University of Berlin wrote to me about a researcher who had been dropped off by parachute near one arrow-like structure. From the air the images looked like gigantic green lines:

> *"They stood out from the white/brown/light-green subsoil like dark green drains. Depending on the season, the area can be covered by sparse steppe grass, thorny bushes and white-bluish inner-Asian wormwood of the*

'Dschusan' species. Then the area dries out again, and at this point the dark green lines begin to glow like monstrous signals toward the heavens. But nothing can be seen on the ground. The parachutist, once landed, crawled around the landscape, but was not able to pick up that he was in the immediate vicinity of one of the 'arrows'. The men in the plane guided their colleague on the ground along a line by using radio. Only then, once he was standing directly on top of it, could he make out the dead straight course across a few hundred metres."

The researchers measured the shapes. On average the base lines ran to 400–600m (1,200ft–1,800ft); the adjacent distance to the triangle at the tip amounted to 800–900m (2,400–3,600ft), and the concluding triangle added another 400m (1,200ft) of length. In total, such a structure could have a length of more than 1.4km (just under 1 mile). The triangles at the apex are isosceles, but the individual corners point in different directions. Markings traced on the ground consisted of piles of stones, and excavations revealed several layers of civilization. In the deepest layer, archaeologists unearthed stone tools from the fourth and third millennia BCE.

Inevitably, researchers and archaeologists wanted answers and explanations. And, as usual, they turned first to those solutions that were close to hand. So, it was suggested that the whole thing was a "fenced-off reserve for large-scale hunting". In this context you might think of steppe asses or antelopes, but this doesn't make any sense

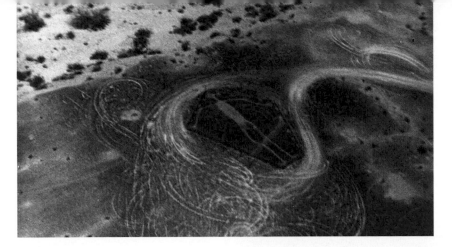

Figures 149–150: Figures near Blythe, California.

in such a dry landscape. Other potential explanations contradict each other, so we end up as perplexed as we might be when considering the meaning of the Nazca lines. At least Peru has mountains from where the images on the desert floor can be viewed. The Ustyurt Plateau has no such elevated area. Dr Vladimir Awinski, a member of the former Soviet Academy of Sciences, told me personally that he considered the shapes to be messages intended for ETs.

And there's more, far away on the other side of the world. To the southeast of Los Angeles, in the USA, not far from the small town of Blythe on the Colorado River, lie scraped in the earth large figures of humans and animals **(Figures 149–150)**.

Figures 151–153: Figures in the Atacama Desert, Chile.

From the Colorado River back down towards Mexico, from the Rocky Mountains to the Appalachians on the northern side of the USA, you can find around 5,000 (yes, five thousand!) of these so-called picture hills that carry bison, birds, snakes, bears, lizards and human beings. Some of these hills contain tombs, but the images themselves are visible only from the air.

In the desert landscape of Macahui on the Mexican–Californian border, there are ground drawings that defy all explanation, covering an area of at least 400 square kilometres (155 square miles). There are circles and wheels as far as the eye can see, just like in far-away Jordan, but also half moons and interlocking rings, and beings surrounded by depictions of light. These images are north of the road that leads from Tijuana to Mexico – or about 25km (15½ miles) from Mexicali toward Tijuana. Aerial photographs are barely possible because bushes have grown all over the land markings, which are also situated on the heavily guarded border zone. It's not like anyone can just take a stroll around there.

Signs for the Celestial Ones

In the Peruvian province of Arequipa, the whole desert floor around Majes and Sihuas teems with geoglyphs from pre-Inca times. The same applies to the Pampa of San José, south of the Nazca plain. And of course to the Atacama Desert in Chile **(Figures 151–153)**.

Covering an area of 40 square kilometres (15 square miles) in the Kalahari Desert, near Verneukpan, South Africa, the latest discovery – thanks to the deployment of satellites – reveals countless spirals and kilometre-long lines running parallel to one another, as well as gigantic triangles and circular arcs.

The geoglyphs in Nazca, Peru, are oversized pictures and gigantic lines. The longest of the broad lines, named *las pistas* (the tracks) by the locals, measures 3.8km ($2^{1}/_{3}$ miles). The longest of the narrow lines reaches 23km (14 miles). They run perfectly straight across deserts and mountains.

Throughout the world, then, people who were not in touch with one another – who, in fact, knew nothing about each other – positioned huge pictures on the ground. Did they all have the same obsession? Or the same need?

I have given updates on the Nazca phenomenon 20 times now and devoted an entire book to this Peruvian mystery [49]. So, while this is not the place to repeat all my theories and findings, I would like to take this opportunity to summarize what the geoglyphs of Nazca are not. They are not:

- An astronomical calendar
- Totem images of the indigenous peoples
- A water-god cult
- A mountain-god cult
- An agricultural cult

- Agricultural plots
- Boundary markings
- Pens for keeping in animals
- Tracks for sacred rituals
- Processional paths
- Repositories for geometrical information
- Reproductions of mirages
- An oversized weaving workshop
- A map
- A cultural atlas
- A pre-Inca Olympia
- A balloon take-off site for the indigenous peoples
- An orgy of mixed-up cultures

Every few years a new book about the Nazca lines appears, and every few years a new TV documentary. Those who don't have the faintest idea about the worldwide phenomenon of geoglyphs on the Earth's surface constantly contradict my theories. And – it's almost getting boring now – most documentary films misrepresent me or attribute to me ideas I've never spoken nor written about. A prime example of this is the documentary by the German archaeologist Dr Markus Reindel, in which my own appearance is cut short, accompanied by the claim that I believe that Nazca is a spaceport for aliens. Either the filmmakers have never read my book *Arrival of the Gods* [49] or they have lied. The first attitude is unscientific and the second dishonest.

On 8 November 63BCE, the Roman consul Marcus Tullius Cicero delivered his celebrated Catiline Oration before the Senate in Rome. Every high school student who has had to memorize this speech will never forget the first sentence:

"Quo usque tandem abutere, Catilina, patientia nostra?", meaning *"When, O Catiline, do you mean to cease abusing our patience?"*

Similarly, I now ask: how long, oh scholars, will you go on thinking in such a one-dimensional way? When will you finally grasp the global nature of the Nazca phenomenon? It can't really be true that the many thousands of geoglyphs in Syria, Jordan, Saudi Arabia, the USA, Chile, Mexico, the Aral Sea or the Kalahari Desert have no association with Nazca in Peru. The "ideology" of our ancient ancestors was the same worldwide. It was always a matter of making signs to the gods, of signalling to those who were moving through the skies. And how long will it take before you finally acknowledge the old texts – those that tell of prehistoric aviation – in your own theories? The figures on the ground have counterpart in ancient literature. The connections between the global signals for the gods and the descriptions in the "holy" books are self-evident. Here are some examples:

The flying machines of the gods are mentioned at length in ancient Indian literature. The Vedas are rich with different types of aircraft, all controlled by pilots [93, 94]. However, as at that time the technology for the manufacture of any type of aircraft did not exist on the Earth, the flying vehicles, the so-called *vimanas*, all originated without exception with the gods. And they, in turn, controlled not just those types of flying machines that could travel only within the Earth's atmosphere, but also others that could journey into the rest of the cosmos. And what did these gods, the extraterrestrials, really want with us all those thousands of years ago? The answer is in the Sabhaparva, a book from the Indian epic the Mahabharata. Chapter 11 (verses 1–4) explains succinctly that the "heavenly ones" came here to study humanity.

The same story is told in the book of the prophet Enoch, who lived before the Great Flood and reports back as an eyewitness – using the first person – on his visit to the "Watchers of the Heavens" in the skies [16]. Exactly the same is described in the Kebra Negast, the 14th-century Ethiopian Book of Kings [95]. The tale is told there of the flight from Jerusalem to Ethiopia:

"So Solomon covered in his flying car in one day a journey that normally takes three months. Without illness and suffering, without hunger and thirst. Without sweat and weariness" (Kebra Negast, Chapter 58).

The usual Nazca interpreters have no idea of the works of al-Mas'ūdī (895–956ce), the Arab world's most significant geographer and encyclopedic chronicler. He writes that Solomon had at his disposal a map showing "the heavenly bodies, the stars, the Earth with its continents and seas, the inhabited lands, their plants and animals, and many other amazing things" [96].

India's greatest poet, Kalidasa, described in his work *Raghuvamsa* the history of the ancient Raghu dynasty. In Song 13 (verses 1–79), he recounts a flight from Lanka to Ayodhya in minute detail and with meticulous accuracy [97]. The flying machine passes the River Godavari, the hermitage of Agastya, the mountains of Chitrakuta, the holy refuge of Atri on the Ganges, and so on – overall a description of a flight covering 2,900km (1,798 miles) from Sri Lanka to Ayodhya in Northern India. When King Dushyanta stepped out of the aircraft, he realized to his bewilderment that although the wheels were turning, they did not stir up any dust. In addition, they were not touching the ground, although Rama was standing on a metal staircase. Matali, one of the pilots, explained the situation to the king. The difference was that this time they had used a heavenly vehicle designed to travel in space, rather than a vehicle intended for Earth's atmosphere.

The ancient texts continually express this distinction with great clarity. Again, the Mahabharata gives us Arjuna's journey into Heaven. Our hero, Arjuna, flies out with Matali, the pilot. Even before the start, Arjuna notices vehicles incapable of flight, still on the ground, and others that were hovering above the take-off area [98]:

"... and, with Matali, Indra's celestial chariot suddenly arrived in a blaze of light, chasing away the darkness and illuminating the clouds, filling the area with turmoil, like the thunder .... When he approached the area, which was invisible to mortals, to those who wander the Earth, he saw heavenly vehicles, utterly

Figure 154: Complex figures in the Nazca Desert, Peru.

beautiful, by the thousand. Up there the sun does not shine, the moon does not shine, but what is seen below on the Earth shines there in its own brilliance. Even from a great distance they look like lamps, but in fact they are vast bodies."

And this is just a small excerpt from ancient literature. Those who know nothing about *vimanas*, nothing about the Tibetan "pearls in the sky", nothing about the flying sun discs of Egypt, nothing about the Biblical Enoch, nothing about the markings on the ground in Jordan, Saudi Arabia, Ustyurt, North America, Mexico, Chile, and so on, should not pass judgment on Nazca.

The figures in the desert of Nazca are not merely random geoglyphs, *pistas* and *lineas*, but have geometrical and mathematical meaning **(Figures 154–155)**. No explanation that relates to agriculture, animal pens, boundary markings, sports grounds and so on, is sufficient. How can you get past those pilots of antiquity?

Figure 155: Complex figures in the Nazca Desert.

There remain tens of thousands of images on the ground, all over the world. They are without doubt designed to be recognizable from the air. They are signs for the celestial ones. In my archive are some 4,000 photos of Nazca. **Figures 155–195** are taken from this series and have, for the most part, never been published anywhere before. There were pictures that were never shown on TV, because a fleeting look on a screen isn't enough. We should take the time to properly examine the "impossible" Nazca evidence. The following aerial photographs show narrow and wide lines criss-crossing each other. We can make out four *pistas*, one behind the other, all pointing in the same direction. There are points in the terrain where *pistas* and *lineas* run together from all sides, like rays from the sun. Anyone who, faced with this mind-boggling visual material, still talks about processional paths, a balloon take-off area, an astronomical calendar or animal pens is talking nonsense. These "scientific" interpretations are really not scientific at all.

Figures 156–195: Figures at Nazca (images mostly published for the first time here).

Figure 157

Figure 158

Figure 159

Figure 160

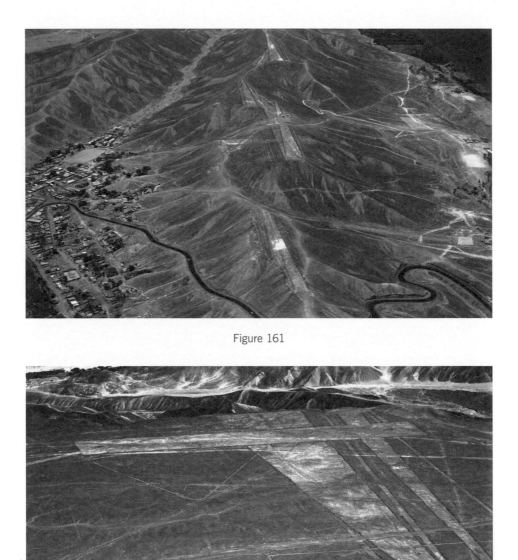

Figure 161

Figure 162

Figure 163

Figure 164

Figure 165

181

Figure 166

Figure 167

Figure 168

Figure 169

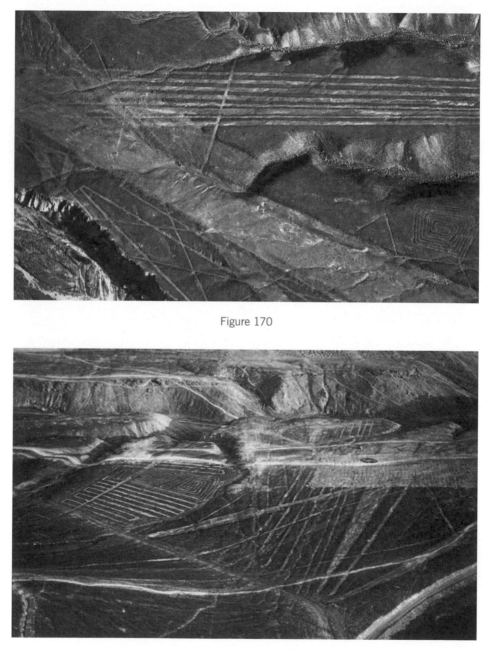

Figure 170

Figure 171

Figure 172

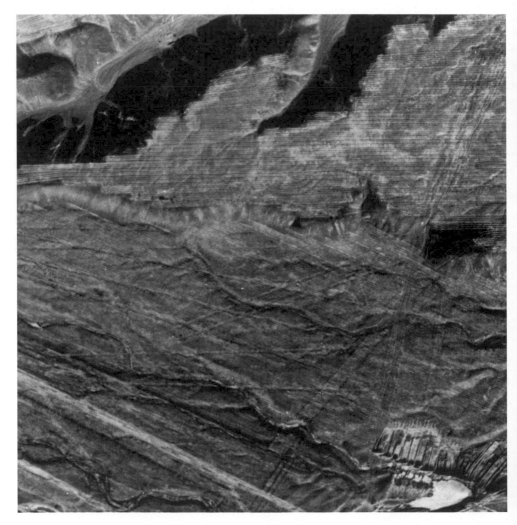

Figure 173

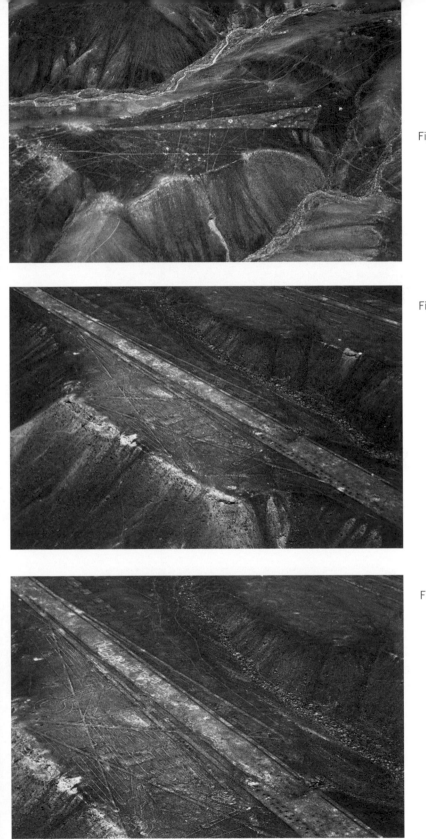

Figure 174

Figure 175

Figure 176

Figure 177

Figure 178

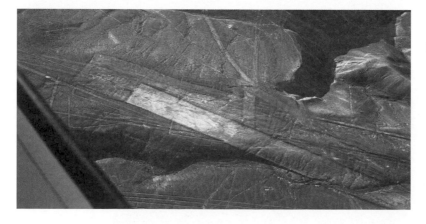

Figure 179

Figure 180

Figure 181

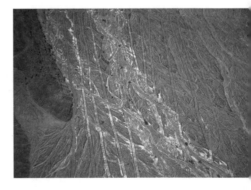

Figure 182

Figure 183

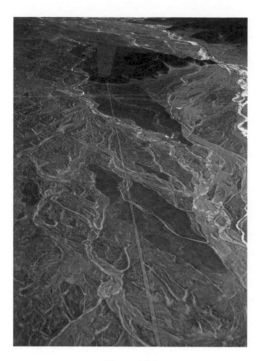

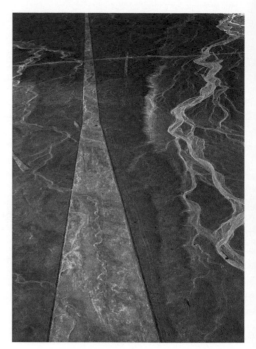

Figure 184

Figure 185

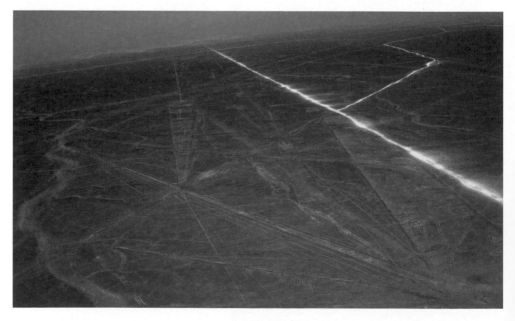

Figure 186

Figure 187

Figure 188

Figure 189

Figure 190

Figure 191

Figure 192

Figure 193

Figure 194

Figure 195

CHAPTER SIX:

One Proof Will Suffice

In the first chapter of my book *Twilight of the Gods* [91] I looked at the ruins of the Puerto del Sol and Puma Punku at Tiahuanaco in the highlands of Bolivia. The subject of my writing was the existence of the megalithic blocks, the enormous platforms, calendar theories and the differing opinions of the experts. I looked at the possible datings and finally at the testimony of the Spanish conquistadors, who around the middle of the 16th century stood before all these mysteries. The consensus has been that these Bolivian enigmas were created by pre-Colombian civilizations. However, I claimed in my book that several of the blocks from Tiahuanaco could not have been created by the people of that era. The work that went into them is consistent with our high-tech civilization and its tools. And this is the reason why we can disprove the theory that our world shows a consistent, linear evolution of technology.

The only responses I got to my book directly were from colleagues – who were, as you would expect, of the same opinion as me. When, on the other hand, I discussed the inconsistencies of Puma Punku and Tiahuanaco with other experts and showed them the revealing pictures, I was met with a disarming shrug of the shoulders with the

Figure 196: Drilled diorite block
at Puma Punku, Tiahuanaco, Bolivia.

usual "Yes, but …!" They would rather drown in their own "buts" than admit that they might not have been fully informed about Puma Punku, or the Puerto del Sol, or that they had never seen the pictures before. And they would never confess to having changed their opinion. I have to accept that I will never fulfil my hope of a generation of experts admitting a change of heart. After all, no scholar will contradict the views of a colleague. In which case everything stays as it was, from one generation to the next. I have also looked in vain for courage from the media, but overall I haven't found it. So, only by using examples from the world of engineering can I prove that the theories we have presented to us about everything in Tiahuanaco being pre-Colombian are unsustainable.

At the site itself is a diorite block around 1m (3ft) high. Diorite is a plutonic rock with a degree of hardness measuring 8 according to the Mohs scale **(Figure 196)**. As a point of comparison, this is the hardness attributed to granite. In order to be able to work diorite with great precision, we need to use tools with a higher degree of hardness (see page 35), such as those made out of diamond. In this block of diorite, a groove 6mm (¼in) wide and nearly 8mm (⅓in) deep runs from top to bottom. In the groove are small holes, drilled there at regular intervals.

No ancient tool could have drawn this groove into the diorite block. Every work utensil from the pre-Colombian era was wide at the back and narrow at the front, tapering to a point. The stonemasons had to hit the wide end with a hammer. Thus they would have hammered the uppermost lips, the edges of the groove, into pieces again and again, and tiny parts would have splintered off. The right angle of the cut is not compatible with a tool that tapers. It has to have been milled, which is something that did not exist in ancient times.

The engineers at Puma Punku have equipped various dressed stones with recesses, edges and grooves **(Figure 197)**. This is because the blocks had to fit into their counterparts with millimetres of precision.

Figure 197: Dressed stone at Puma Punku, Tiahuanaco.

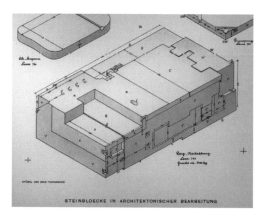

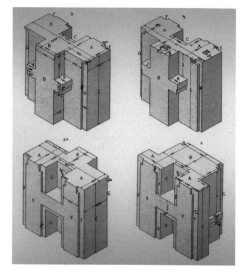

Figure 198: Precisely carved diorite block at Puma Punku.

Figure 199: Four prefabricated diorite building blocks.

The block in **Figure 198** is rectangular, 2.74m (8ft) long and 1.57m (5ft) wide. It has six faces: top, bottom and four sides. There are various subdivisions on these six faces, which appear in rectangular and square forms. On the front side – on the right in the image – are a larger square and two smaller squares, one on top of the other, marked with the letter "P". Just try cutting, filing or hammering out these precise squares with a chisel! I live in the Swiss mountains, where people also work with granite, not just for gravestones, but for the military, too. I showed the pictures to five specialists and asked their advice. "It can't be done with Stone Age tools" was the unanimous reply. On the uppermost face of the block, pretty much at the midpoint of the left edge, there are two recesses next to each other – a rectangle and beside it a notch or a plug. Stone Age hammers could make neither of these. In addition, the entire block is shaped like a wedge, with the back thicker than the front. Every small detail provides evidence that painstaking planning was necessary to create such a precision piece of engineering. Ultimately every recess, square and rectangle has to fit into its counterpart. Seamlessly. The total weight of the block by the way comes to 8,500kg (18,740lb).

Figure 199 shows four diorite blocks, which at first glance appear identical, but they are not. Every single block is an exceptional individual achievement. They are prefabricated elements functioning as two halves that can be pushed together, rather like LEGO© building blocks today. Accurate to the millimetre, the measurement on the rails, recesses and cross beams, as well as the precise details, provides evidence of engineering calculations that must have happened before the work began. But where would those calculations have been written down? On coca or corn leaves? On skins? In the sand? Through scratching on stone? In laid-out twine? What measuring tape was there marked up in millimetres? This sort of precision work would be impossible to chisel out in an impromptu way. One single wrong blow, and the whole piece of work would be ruined. Which engineering school might these ancient architects have visited? Where did their technical measurement devices come from? What about their knowledge about the particular hardness of the various dressed stones? Which workshop did the stencils come from? Who built the craning devices they would have needed?

Today, skilled craftsmen carry out work like this using milling and drilling tools, each with a point harder than the stones themselves, working at a high rotational speed. The machines are guided over steel templates to ensure accuracy. The lifting or crane devices had to turn the finished individual parts and lock them into each other without the slightest fragmentation of the material and taking into account the different surfaces, rectangles, squares, recesses, ledges and indentations. Comparatively speaking, the construction methods and machinery of our time must be much more primitive than the technology used thousands of years ago in Tiahuanaco.

One doctor of archaeology, a brilliant and humorous scholar who saw my pictures, laughed cheerfully in my face. "Erich," he said, "you have fallen for a fake. Some scholar wanted to make fun of you in front of his students. So they drafted the technical drawings and pushed them in your direction. The whole thing is a practical joke."

However, the drawings shown here, together with the letters added to them and the millimetre measurements, are taken from a book by Max Uhle (1856–1944) and Alfons Stübel (1835–1904). Uhle was an archaeologist, often referred to as the "father of Peruvian archaeology". Alphons Stübel was a geologist. They worked for a year and a half in the highlands of Bolivia, recording the exact measurements and descriptions of the blocks. Their work, *The Ruins of Tiahuanaco in the Highlands of Ancient Peru* [99], appeared in 1892. That is:

Eighteen hundred and ninety two.

If this is the year Tiahuanaco's extraordinary feats of engineering appeared, the joke is on them!

BIBLIOGRAPHY

[1] Tello, Julio, C.: "Discovery of the Chavin Culture in Peru" in *American Antiquity*, Vol. IX. No. 1, Menasha, 1943

[2] Däniken, Erich von: *Astronaut Gods of the Maya*. Vermont, 2017

[3] Stingl, Miloslav: *Die Inkas – Ahnen der Sonnensöhne*. Düsseldorf, 1978

[4] Disselhoff, H. D.: *Das Imperium der Inka*. Berlin, 1972

[5] Pörtner, Rudolf und Davies, Nigel: "Alte Kulturen der Neuen Welt" *Neue Erkenntnisse der Archäologie*. Düsseldorf, 1980

[6] Trimborn, Hermann: *Das Alte Amerika*. Stuttgart, 1959

[7] Nachtigall, Horst: *Die amerikanischen Megalithkulturen*. Berlin, 1958

[8] Huber, Siegfried: *In the Realm of the Inca*. Hale, 1959

[9] Katz, Friedrich: *Ancient American Civilizations*. Munich, 1969

[10] Franz, Heinrich: "Tiermaske und Mensch-Tier-Verwandlung als Grundmotive der altamerikanischen Kunst" in *Jahrbuch des kunsthistorischen Instituts der Universität Graz*, 1975

[11] Wedemeyer, Inge von: *Sonnengott und Sonnenmenschen*. Tübingen, 1970

[12] Volkrodt, Wolfgang: *Es war ganz anders. Die intelligente Technik der Vorzeit*. München, 1991

[13] Brugsch, Heinrich: *Die Sage von der geflügelten Sonnenscheibe nach altägyptischen Quellen*. Göttingen, 1870

[14] Rießler, P.: *Altjüdisches Schrifttum außerhalb der Bibel. Die Apokalypse des Abraham*. Augsburg, 1928

[15] Kanjilal, Dileep Kumar: *Vimanas in Ancient India*. Calcutta, 1985

[16] Kautzsch, Emil: *Die Apokryphen und Pseudepigraphen des Alten Testaments*, Band II: *Das Buch Henoch*. Tübingen, 1900

[17] Krickeberg, Walter: *Pre-Colombian Ancient Religions*. London, 1968

[18] Burckhardt, Georg: *Gilgamesch: eine Erzählung aus dem Alten Orient*. Munich, 1920

[19] *Die Heilige Schrift*. Stuttgart, 1972

[20] Däniken, Erich von: *History is Wrong*. New Jersey, 2009

[21] Bopp, Franz: *Ardschuna's Reise zu Indra's Himmel: nebst anderen Episoden des Mahabharata*. Berlin, 1824

[22] The Book of Mormon

[23] Talmage, James E.: *Articles of Faith*. Salt Lake City

[24] Kauffmann Doig, Federico: "La cultura Chavin" in *Las grandes civilizaciones del antiguo Perú*, Tomo III. Lima, 1963

[25] *Kebra Negast, die Herrlichkeit der Könige; Abhandlungen der philosophisch-philologischen Klasse der Königlich-Bayrischen Akademie der Wissenschaften*. Hrsg. Carl Bezold. Volume 23, Section 1, Munich, 1905

[26] Däniken, Erich von: *Remnants of the Gods*. New Jersey, 2013

[27] Stöpel, Karl Theodor: *Südamerikanische prähistorische Tempel und Gottheiten*. Frankfurt, 1912

[28] Preuss, Theodor: *Monumentale vorgeschichtliche Kunst*. Göttingen, 1929

[29] Lechtmann, Haether: "Vorkolumbianische Oberflächenveredelung von Metall" in *Spektrum der Wissenschaft*. August, 1984

[30] Däniken, Erich von: *Arrival of the Gods*. Munich, 1997

[31] De la Vega, Inca Garcilaso: *Comentarios Reales de los Incas*. Madrid, 1722

[32] Molina, Cristóbal de: *Relación de las fábulas y ritos de los incas*. Hamburg

[33] Betanzanos, Juan de: *Suma y narration de los Incas*, Volume 1. Madrid, 1880

[34] Caillois, Roger: *The Writing of Stones*. 1988

[35] Disselhoff, Hans-Dietrich: *Das Imperium der Inka und die indianischen Frühkulturen der Andenländer*. Berlin, 1972

[36] Grömling, Willi: *Tibets altes Geheimnis. Gesar, ein Sohn des Himmels*. Groß-Gerau, 2005

[37] Hamilton, Edith: *Plato – The Collected Dialogues*. Princeton, 1961. Gregory, Andrew: *Timaeus and Critias*. Oxford, 2008

[38] Muck, Otto: *Secret of Atlantis*. Glasgow, 1978

[39] Galanopoulos, Angelos and Bacon, Edward: *Atlantis: The Truth Behind The Legend*. Munich, 1977

[40] Nestke, Fritz und Riemer Thomas: *Atlantis – ein Kontinent taucht auf*. Halver, 1988

[41] Däniken, Erich von: *Odyssey of the Gods*. Munich, 1999

[42] Kruparz, Heinrich: *Atlantis und Lemuria*. Gnas, 2009

[43] Churchward, James: *The Children of Mu*. New York, 1968

[44] Blumrich, Josef: *Kásskara und die sieben Welten*. Vienna and Düsseldorf, 1979

[45] Däniken, Erich von: *Remnants of the Gods*. New Jersey, 2013

[46] Däniken, Erich von: *Grüße aus der Steinzeit.* Rottenburg, 2010

[47] Däniken, Erich von: *Die Steinzeit war ganz anders.* Munich, 1991

[48] Fosar, Grazyna und Bludorf, Franz: "Gottes Landkarte. Russische Wissenschaftler fanden 120 Millionen altes Artefakt", Internet Article (http://www.fosar-bludorf.com/ural)

[49] Däniken, Erich von: *Arrival of the Gods.* Munich, 1997

[50] Däniken, Erich von: *Von Däniken's Proof: Further Astonishing Evidence of Man's Extraterrestrial Origins,* New York, 1978

[51] Dougherty, Cecil N.: *Valley of the Giants.* Cleburne, Texas, 1971

[52] Cremo, Michael A. and Thompson, Richard L.: *Forbidden Archaeology.* Florida, 1993

[53] Ruzo, Daniel: *La Historia fantastica de un descubrimiento.* Mexico, 1974

[54] *Las Ultimas Noticias,* Santiago de Chile, 26 October 1968

[55] Eissmann, Rafael Videla: *El Enladrillado, una meseta prediluvial en los Andes.* Santiago de Chile, 2008

[56] Kiss, Edmund: *Das Sonnentor von Tihuanaku und Hörbigers Welteislehre.* Leipzig, 1937

[57] Flindt, Max H.: *Between the Apes and the Angels.* Los Altos, 1999

[58] "Drei Scheiben als Beweise für die Götter-Astronauten?" in *Kärntner Tageszeitung,* 1 July 1977

[59] "Spuren aus dem Weltall?" in *Salzburger Nachrichten,* 26 June 1977

[60] Childress, David H.: "The Evidence for Ancient Atomic Warfare", Part 1 (Extracted from *Nexus Magazine,* Vol. 7, No. 5, Aug.–Sept, 2000)

[61] "Dating the Lybian Desert Silica-Glass" in *Nature,* No.170, 1952

[62] "5000-year-old mummy has an artificial heart" in *Weekly World News,* 22 June 1986

[63] Letter from Dr Milan Kalous to Erich von Däniken. EvD Archiv., No. 003276

[64] Pooyard, Patrice: *Revelation of the Pyramids.* Universum-Film, Munich, 2011

[65] Bodnaruk, Nikolai: "The Mysterious Net across the Globe" in *Komsomolskaya Pravda,* and later republished in *Sputnik* (Digest of the Soviet Press), 9/1974

[66] Glasenapp, Helmuth von: *Der Jainismus. Eine indische Erlösungsreligion.* Hildesheim, 1984 (Original Edition 1925)

[67] Frauwallner, Erich: *Geschichte der indischen Philosophie.* Salzburg, 1953

[68] Krannich, Paul H.: *Henochs Uhr.* Norderstedt, 2009

[69] Wahrmund, A.: *Diodor von Sicilien. Geschichtsbibliothek,* Book One. Stuttgart, 1866

[70] Roth, Rudolf von: *Über den Mythos von den fünf Menschengeschlechtern bei Hesiod und die indische Lehre von den vier Weltaltern.* Tübingen, 1860

[71] Stuart, David and George: *Palenque, Eternal City of the Maya.* London, 2008

[72] Schomerus, H.W.: *Indische und christliche Enderwartung und Erlösungshoffnung.* Gütersloh, 1941

[73] Feer, Léon: *Anales du Musée Guimet. Extraits du Kandjour.* Paris, 1882

[74] "Der Mensch stammt doch ab" in *Focus,* No.44/1996

[75] "Darwin ja – aber Gott sorgte für den Urknall" (Interview with Susanne Stettler) in *Der Blick,* 28 October 1996

[76] Chardin, Teilhard de: *Man's Place in Nature.* Glasgow, 1966

[77] Puccetti, Roland: *Außerirdische Intelligenz.* Düsseldorf, 1970

[78] Flindt, Max: *Mankind, Child of the Stars.* Greenwich, Con., 1974

[79] Wilder-Smith, A. E.: *God: To Be or Not to Be.* Heerbrugg, 1976

[80] Hoyle, Fred: *The Intelligent Universe.* London. 1983 and Hoyle, Fred and Wickramasinghe, Chandra: *Evolution From Space.* Littlehampton,1981

[81] Crick, Francis: *Life Itself.* New York, 1981

[82] Vollmert, Bruno: *Das Molekül und das Leben.* Reinbeck, 1985

[83] Horn, Arthur D. and Mallory-Horn, Lynette A.: *Humanity's Extraterrestrial Origins: ET Influence on Humankind's Biological and Cultural Evolution.* 1977

[84] Nagel, Thomas: *Mind and Cosmos: Why the Materialist Neo-Darwinian Conception of Nature is Almost Certainly False.* Oxford, 2012

[85] Streeck, Nina: "Glaubenskrieg um Darwin". In: *Neue Zürcher Zeitung,* 7 July 2013

[86] Soto, Alvaro: *Buritaca 200 – Cuidad Perdida.* Bogota

[87] Preuss, Theodor Konrad: *Forschungsreise zu den Kagaba.* Vienna, 1926

[88] Sandars, N. K.: *The Epic of Gilgamesh.* Baltimore, 1960

[89] Burckhardt, George: *Gilgamesch, eine Erzählung aus dem Alten Orient.* Frankfurt, 1958

[90] Kautsch, Emil: *Die Apokryphen und Epigraphen des alten Testaments,* Band II: Buch Henoch

[91] Däniken, Erich von: *Twilight of the Gods.* Rottenburg, 2009

[92] "The Mysterious Arrows of Ustyurt" in *Soviet Culture,* 11 August 1989

[93] Gentes, Lutz: *Die Wirklichkeit der Götter – Raumfahrt im frühen Indien.* Munich, 1996

[94] Kanjilal, Dileep Kumar: *Vimanas in Ancient India.* Calcutta, 1985

[95] *Kebra Negast, die Herrlichkeit der Könige; Abhandlungen der philosophisch-philologischen Klasse der Königlich- Bayrischen Akademie der Wissenschaften.* Hrsg. Carl Bezold. Vol. 23, Section 1, Munich, 1905

[96] Al-Mas-'udi: *To the Edges of the Earth*

[97] Bopp, Franz: *Ardschuna's Reise zu Indra's Himmel: nebst anderen Episoden des Mahabharata.* Berlin, 1824

[98] Roy, Chandra Pratap: *The Mahabharata, Volume: Drona Parva.* Calcutta, 1888

[99] Stübel, A. und Uhle, M.: *Die Ruinenstätte von Tiahuanaco im Hochlande des alten Peru.* Leipzig, 1892

[100] Däniken, Erich von: *Pathways to the Gods: The Stones of Kiribati.* New York, 1983

[101] Däniken, Erich von: *The Gods and their Grand Design.* London, 1984

[102] Däniken, Erich von: *Chariots of the Gods?.* London, 1990

PICTURE CREDITS

Figures 5–12, 25 and 26: Mario Gigandet, Guatemala

Figures 36–37: Dr Wolfgang Volkrodt

Figures 71–72: Floyd Varesi, Gelterkinden

Figures 107–108: Shun Daichi/Kenichi Shindo

Figure 120: De Viaje por Argentina

Figure 140: Google Earth

Figures 141–146 (Drawings): Ramon Zürcher, Heimenschwand

All other illustrations:
© Erich von Däniken
CH-3803-Beatenberg, Switzerland

INDEX

Page numbers in *italics* refer to illustrations